"Fiona Robertson's succinct volume is a personal guide to the Living Inquiries, the self-liberation method of which she is a highly adept facilitator. She shows us how fearless and open inquiry can free us of the 'seeming self,' the illusory yet powerful tyrant that keeps us stuck in a limited world with limited possibilities."

—**Gabor Maté, MD**, author of *In the Realm of Hungry Ghosts*, *When the Body Says No*, and *Scattered*, and coauthor of *Hold On to Your Kids*

"*The Art of Finding Yourself* by Fiona Robertson offers a cornucopia of information and wisdom about awakening and the Living Inquiries. Read it straight through or pick a chapter at random and the result will be the same—an insightful 'aha' moment, a shift in perception, or a dropping into the direct experience of that which she points to. *The Art of Finding Yourself* is a great little read—which could quite possibly lead to a great BIG change."

—**J. Stewart Dixon**, author, teacher, and founder of Blue Collar Enlightenment

"*The Art of Finding Yourself* is an immensely helpful and practical guide to dismantling our identification with our stories, staying fully present with our denied and difficult underlying emotions, and learning to rest in natural curiosity and awareness, in full acceptance of whatever arises. Fiona's personal vulnerability and profound clarity shine throughout her book, which I highly recommend."

—**Susan Thesenga**, spiritual teacher, author of *The Undefended Self* and *Love Unbroken*, mother and grandmother, and cofounder, with her husband Donovan, of Sevenoaks Retreat Center in Madison, VA

"Fiona Robertson's work is at the leading edge of the marriage of Eastern spirituality with Western psychotherapy. Deep spirituality can so easily become a way for people to avoid the psychological challenges of life, but *The Art of Finding Yourself* is a book that makes spirituality real, taking it right into our pain, where it can have its greatest effect."

—**Tim Freke**, deep life philosopher and author of
Deep Awake

The Art of Finding Yourself

Live Bravely and Awaken to
Your True Nature

FIONA ROBERTSON

NON-DUALITY PRESS
An Imprint of New Harbinger Publications

Publisher's Note

This publication is designed to provide accurate and authoritative information in regard to the subject matter covered. It is sold with the understanding that the publisher is not engaged in rendering psychological, financial, legal, or other professional services. If expert assistance or counseling is needed, the services of a competent professional should be sought.

Distributed in Canada by Raincoast Books

Copyright © 2016 by Fiona Robertson
        Non-Duality Press
        An imprint of New Harbinger Publications, Inc.
        5674 Shattuck Avenue
        Oakland, CA 94609
        www.newharbinger.com

Cover design by Amy Shoup

Library of Congress Cataloging-in-Publication Data on file

18   17   16

10   9   8   7   6   5   4   3   2   1   First Printing

Contents

Foreword

Since developing the Living Inquiries with the help of many skillful facilitators, including Fiona Robertson, I have encountered great difficulty expressing just how transformative they have been in my own life. Mostly, words come up empty.

Those who have followed my teachings through the years can see that a fairly abrupt change happened around 2010, when the Inquiries first became available to the public. I had been using the Inquiries for a number of years on my own before making them public. I had seen such powerful shifts in perception that my previous way of speaking about non-duality and spiritual awakening was essentially obliterated. The Inquiries had put everything on the chopping block—my self, others, the world, and reality—but especially the grand, spiritual concepts such as awareness, oneness, true nature, all of it.

Everything was totally burned up with the Inquiries. I lost my vocabulary. I was so grateful for this loss because it left me with nowhere to stand, as I was no longer able to be the authority on any statement of what is true and real in an objective sense.

After this period of exploration, as a teacher, I made a 180-degree shift. No longer could I sit in front of the room with a straight face at a *satsang* and pronounce truth. I was stripped totally naked. I had nothing to offer. I saw that even offering that was pretending to offer something. Now, you might say that this looks like nihilism. But it was nothing like that. It was about truly coming into my own experience, embracing it fully, loving and accepting it all—including all the imperfections. It was about being fully human, feeling everything while also moving beyond all of it. It was an embrace of awakening; then awakening out of that awakening; then awakening out of the idea that I could ever teach something that elusive.

Having lost the ability to even say things like, "There is no self" (an assumption that had also become toast through the Inquiries), I was left with nothing to teach. Frankly, the entire enterprise of spiritual teaching felt like a big game of nonsense. I stopped being able to make objective, blanket statements about what is true and real—about anything. I stopped being able to say "I'm done" or "I have attained perfect enlightenment," because I also saw those to be completely empty statements that are only interesting to an ego that takes itself to be real.

I moved freely within the ever-deepening flow that showed up through the Living Inquiries, noticing that there is no end to the depth of freedom. Nowhere to stand. No plateau from which to teach. My life became just about enjoying my life. Plain and simple. I continued to help people, but I focused on very human issues like addiction, anxiety, depression, and deficiency stories. In my own journey, I found that focusing on those points made all the difference. All that I have been able to sincerely say to people since 2010 is, "Are you ready to look?"

Having watched this transformation in my life, I have noticed that very few people take the Living Inquiries this deeply. It takes courage, lots of it. It takes patience. It takes being aware and letting everything be, letting it all be explored with a few simple questions. Many don't want to go there. They want to find some plateau and hold onto it, some comfortable spiritual framework, some mental understanding, or some assumptions about themselves, others, the world, reality, or awakening. They want a place to land.

Because the Inquiries do not provide this place to land, many back away before the true depth of this work can be realized. There is no judgment in any of this, for we all do it—we all look for some sense of safety and certainty in our ideas. I have done it. But the Inquiries make it impossible to continue to do that, as long as you do not back away from them.

Fiona Robertson did not back away. She went head-on, as deeply as I have gone with this work. I have watched her incredible skillfulness with clients. I have listened to her clarity and watched her willingness to look at the deepest nooks and crannies of her belief systems. I have seen her collide with deep pain and fear and then open to it, going beyond it with this work. Every time I read something Fiona has written, I quietly nod "yes" to every word and every sentence. She is exploring the way I have explored. She simply remains open to looking and to watching the unravelling of suffering happen quite naturally and without effort.

I do not say all this to put Fiona or myself in some special category of the truly awakened, for that category is also empty. I nod quietly because I see her absolute openness and her unwillingness to land anywhere. Like myself, Fiona's life has become about her own personal experience. She is not out in the world proclaiming objective truths that try to summarize the reality of all humans and place it in one tidy, conceptual box. She is merely expressing how life actually shows up in her humanness and the amazing changes that happen when we are simply ready to look. For me, the only authentic way to express ourselves after using the Inquiries a lot is to express how being human shows up and how moving beyond old patterns of suffering is inevitable when you are looking.

In the end, the Living Inquiries slaughter the teacher within, leaving only the naked humanness. They have slaughtered the teacher within Fiona, leaving only her beautiful, vulnerable humanness and sincere compassion for those who are suffering.

This is why I am writing this foreword. I can write it and sleep soundly at night knowing that I am not endorsing another teacher handing out grand concepts. I am endorsing a human being with incredible skill as a facilitator—a human being who can assist you to look precisely because she has been open to look at everything for herself.

If you are interested in the Living Inquiries, I cannot think of a better way to forge this pathless path than to follow in Fiona's footsteps. Whether you work with her in private or group sessions, read this book, or follow her Facebook posts, you are in great hands. These are hands that you can trust completely. She has nothing to offer except the same invitation I have been offering since 2010: "Are you ready to look?"

She will not lead you astray because she will not lead you at all. She is not teaching you what to know or where to go. Following Fiona's footsteps does not entail mimicking her words or listening to her at the front of some room as the authority on all things. Rather, it is simply following her quiet and humble lead as she looks at her own experience and invites you to look at your own. She is inviting you to explore every assumption on which your suffering is based. This is a mutual dance where there is no authority anywhere in the mix. This book is rich with personal experience. And that's what we all resonate with.

It is with great honor and respect that I introduce you to Fiona, if you are not aware of her. I give you over to her with the hope that you will take her invitation and not land on the many places that one can land on this beautiful journey of freedom. I can't even say that this journey is about finding the deepest peace, acceptance or love that is possible, even though that it surely coming. This is about something more than that, about truly investigating, in the most loving and restful way, what masses of people on earth are running away from—the entirety of their own experience exactly as it shows up in each moment.

Scott Kiloby
March 2015

Introduction

The Living Inquiries are dynamic and deeply personal investigations that dissolve the beliefs, fears, and addictions that often run our lives. By gently allowing our thoughts and feelings to be exactly as they are, and by learning to look, feel, and inquire, we experience a profound release from the emotional and sensory energies of our personal history and the "stories" about ourselves (and others) that hold us back.

When we're willing to investigate our experiences in this way, we discover a relaxation, or sense of okayness, in the midst of whatever is happening. And we experience radical shifts in perspective, no longer seeing ourselves or others as problematic. Our struggles naturally begin to reduce, our suffering becomes less intense, and our relationships become more harmonious. There are five Inquiries; each one enables us to look at ourselves and life from a different perspective.

The Unfindable Inquiry is the inquiry on which all the others are based. It has many uses, including:

Looking at the beliefs we have about ourselves. Many people have low self-esteem, believing themselves to be deficient, lacking, or flawed, while others have an overinflated sense of their qualities, believing themselves to be better or more than others.

Looking at the beliefs we have about other people and the wider world. When we find ourselves triggered by people or events, inquiry helps us unravel the knots of belief and assumption that unconsciously affect us.

Looking at our beliefs about spirituality. For those who are involved in spiritual seeking, the Inquiries offer a way to investigate beliefs about enlightenment, awakening, and other related topics.

The Anxiety Inquiry takes us into the heart of fight-or-flight-or-freeze responses and the perception of threat or danger that gives rise to anxiety, fear, phobias, worry, anger, rage, stress, and trauma. By gently looking and allowing, both mind and body are able to gradually and safely unwind from the mental, emotional, and physical effects of anxieties and traumas that we may have carried for a long time.

The Compulsion Inquiry allows us to investigate and dissolve the push-pull of addiction, compulsion, and obsession. Whatever the object of our desire is—tobacco, drugs, alcohol, food, porn, sex, gambling, online gaming, work, cleaning—we discover what's really running the drives and impulses that we seem powerless to resist.

The Boomerang Inquiry works in tandem with the Unfindable Inquiry, giving us the opportunity to see what unconscious beliefs are in play whenever another person or situation triggers us to judge or react.

The Panorama Inquiry similarly enables us to identify and name the belief or story that's running when we find ourselves triggered and disturbed by a number of people or life situations.

In practice, the Living Inquiries do not have a fixed, rigid format. The flexible, fluid process enables us to inquire into any belief, life circumstance, or experience—however painful or challenging. In sessions, facilitators weave the Inquiries together in a natural and seamless way, allowing clients to deepen their experience. Realizations and insights arise effortlessly and spontaneously. Working with a certified facilitator is highly recommended, as is learning to self-facilitate. Those of us who find the Inquiries transformative are those who are willing to look consistently at whatever arises.

Integral to the Inquiries is what Scott Kiloby calls "Natural Rest." This describes the practice of resting in awareness for short moments throughout the day. When we rest, we repeatedly take a moment to let everything be as it is: we are fully present and aware of our thoughts and bodily feelings or sensations without trying to change, manage, or deal with them. Resting is a cumulative practice; the more we do it, the greater our capacity to be with our experience becomes and we are less and less inclined to try to escape it in some way. Openly allowing our experience creates a greater sense of ease and spaciousness in our lives.

Inquiry, like many other skills, takes practice. What matters most is our willingness to be honest about whatever is here, including resistance and wanting to escape. The inquiry process is gentle, as there is no forcing or pushing and everything is allowed to be exactly as it is in each moment. It is also unflinching, as we delve into our suffering and stuckness in all their forms. Over time, as inquiry becomes part of our lives, our commitment to being present to the truth of the moment increases. We become braver and better able to look at all the aspects of ourselves and our lives that we've been afraid to face.

This book is an invitation to live bravely, moment by moment, and be with your experience in a radically different way. It is an invitation to stop and look, to see what is actually here, to notice that you're not what or who you think you are, to rest in the present, and to experience what lies beyond your beliefs.

In late 2011, Scott Kiloby invited me to train as a facilitator of his newly developed inquiry method. At the time, I was in the process of editing two of his books, *Living Realization* and *The Living Inquiry*, so this seemed like a natural extension of what we were already doing. I said yes without the slightest hesitation. Eight of us embarked on that initial journey with Scott and it took us to places we could never have imagined.

About five years later, so much has happened. We've substantially developed the inquiry process and have worked with thousands of clients from around the world on a huge variety of issues.

We've trained around ninety more facilitators across the United States, Canada, Europe, and Australia. We've held live events in North America, the United Kingdom, and Hungary, in particular. We have a growing, thriving online Living Inquiries community. In early 2014, Scott opened The Kiloby Center for Recovery in Palm Springs, California, bringing a much-needed, new paradigm into the recovery community.

None of this was planned, of course. As we each continued our own explorations with the Inquiries, and began to work with clients, word spread. People from all kinds of backgrounds have found their way to us: some are longtime spiritual seekers; others are simply tired of suffering. Most are discovering, as we have done, that once they begin to inquire, life seems to change. The process itself is straightforward. All it takes is a willingness to look.

Throughout this time, I've been consistently inspired to write about our work. After inquiring for a few months, it began to naturally flow and hasn't stopped since. The writing itself springs from the inquiry process; previously, I'd kept my writing limited to my private journals. Then, every few weeks, I wrote blog posts that have been shared on our various websites. It seems fitting to now share my writing with you as a collection. This book, therefore, is not a how-to manual, but an invitation to begin and continue your own looking. If you're inspired to explore the Inquiries for yourself, there are resources listed at the end of the book.

I can't imagine life without inquiry now. In the early days, I believed that I could, perhaps, use the process to get rid of all my pain and suffering so that I'd become a better version of me. Quickly, and thankfully, that notion was dispelled. To be able to look deeply at all the beliefs, fears, and compulsions that keep me limited and defined as a solid, separate self is an incredible gift. To be able to look directly at whatever is happening in the moment, and let it be exactly as it is, has proved to be radical and transformative. More than any other teaching, method, or practice, it is the Living Inquiries that have brought about the most profound changes in my life, and for that I am truly grateful.

On Believing Ourselves Deficient

For many years, it seemed self-evident that there was something wrong with me. A fundamental sense that I was too much or too little, off-center, not quite right in both definable and indefinable ways, permeated most of my experience. What else could explain the conflict, pain, and discomfort that inevitably arose in my relationships? After yet another scene of tears, shouting, and bewilderment with a boyfriend, I described the pattern in my journal:

> When anger comes at me from someone, from somewhere
> outside of me, at first I'm there: holding, defending,
> blocking. Then I crumble and it starts: "I'm sorry. I'm really,
> really sorry." "It's all my fault." "It would've all been alright
> if I hadn't done, or said, or been."
>
> Very soon, I'm not in myself at all. I'm somewhere else,
> a small, small girl, trying so, so hard to be good and not be
> a problem. I apologize for myself and deny myself and lie
> about myself and betray myself. If you're right (which you
> always are, or at least, you say you are), then I can be
> nothing but wrong.
>
> And so some smallish human mistake, a frailty, some
> misconceived, insensitive, unthinking act of no particular
> consequence becomes an enormous wrongdoing, a hideous,
> heinous crime; suddenly, the whole situation has taken on
> entirely delusionary proportions because I'm apologizing for
> my existence while simultaneously knowing that what's
> happened between us is, actually, just a part of being alive.

Despite the sense that there was something illusory playing out, such occasions seemed to provide all the evidence to prove that there was indeed something wrong with me. Like many of us, I tried hard to make myself better through therapy, remedies, and meditation. New ideas and approaches brought new dawns, followed by the inevitable disappointment that—despite my efforts—I seemed to remain, stubbornly, me.

Stories of deficiency like this appear to be absolutely real. Thoughts, emotions, and sensations create compelling experiences—the validity of which seems certain. We believe that there is something wrong with us simply because our thoughts and emotions tell us so. And we are always able to back up our claims of inadequacy, telling ourselves things like, "Of course I'm a failure, that's why I didn't get the job" or "If I was really okay, I'd be in a long-term relationship by now." We each view the situations and people we encounter through the lens of our own story of deficiency, comparing, contrasting, and coming up short.

It seems paradoxical that there may also be times when we believe that we're better than others. The inner story of deficiency may be so painful that we develop a compensatory persona, projecting the unwanted qualities outward. We think things like, "I'm the strong one, it's him who is weak," or "If only other people would live like I do, the world would be a better place." However, it takes effort to keep up the pretense and we find ourselves quickly defensive, shoring up our identities against attack.

Eventually, exhausted, we may find ourselves incapable of continuing to hold the line of our beliefs. We begin to investigate the truth of what we've believed for so long and start to question the basic assumptions that have underpinned our story of deficiency: that there is a solid, separate "me"; that there is something wrong with "me"; that steps need to be taken to improve "me"; that there is a destination to reach in order for "me" to be okay.

Through the process of inquiring into what we've believed ourselves to be, we discover that we are not who we thought we were. True inquiry allows us to see through the identities and beliefs that we've clung to for so long. We realize that what previously seemed solid and fixed is, in fact, a mere chimera. And as we see that the story of deficiency is just that—a story—our hearts inevitably begin to break open.

Out beyond ideas of wrongdoing and rightdoing, there is a field.
I will meet you there.

　　　　　—Rumi*

---

* Jalal al-Din Rumi, "The Great Wagon," in *The Essential Rumi*, trans. Coleman Barks (San Francisco: HarperOne, 2004).

On Discovering the Resources Within

Many spiritual teachers and traditions talk about finding what we need within ourselves. We're encouraged to look within, rather than seeking salvation outside ourselves. Ultimately, this is great advice. However, if we perceive ourselves to be lacking or deficient, it feels totally counterintuitive. The whole seeking movement—whatever it is we're seeking, be it spiritual sustenance, enlightenment, material possessions, or personal achievements—really emanates from the sense that we're not enough as we are. This sense of lack can be visceral; it can feel like there's an insatiable, unfillable void or black hole right in our center.

The notion of deficiency is at the heart of nearly all the beliefs we have about ourselves. We believe ourselves to be lacking or failing in some, even all, areas of life. It's hardly surprising, then, that we look outside ourselves for things to make up for our perceived shortcomings. In our own eyes, we stand or fall on whether we manage to fill the gap that we feel in the center of ourselves.

The sense of our own deficiency is deeply compelling. In fact, we take it to be fact rather than a matter of belief. We make statements about ourselves like, "I'm not good enough" or "I'm the weak one" or "I'm a victim," as if stating objective truth, because what we believe about ourselves *feels* true. The statements come with images and bodily feelings and sensations; we experience our beliefs in both mind and body.

The bodily feelings often come with labels. Tightness in the chest might be called "anxiety" or "anger." A churning feeling in the stomach may be labeled "anxiety" or "stress." Each of us has our own unique language and we've often taken the bodily sensations and energies to mean something, too. As we inquire, we discover exactly what meanings we've ascribed to each sensation. We gently unravel the entangled words, images, and sensations that we've assumed mean we're deficient in some way. As we begin to look and feel, letting every element be as it is, we often make surprising discoveries. The feeling in the belly that we've been mistaking for weakness all this time turns out to contain strength as well. The sensation in the chest that we were convinced meant that we were irretrievably damaged was actually a simple and natural longing for connection.

So often during sessions, there is a moment when transformation occurs. A previously terrifying image becomes benign. A word that has always held negative meaning turns into a mute collection of letters. A seemingly significant energy begins to move or change—and the meaning we've ascribed to it disperses into the ether.

It would appear that nothing can be present without its seeming opposite being somewhere in the mix, even if it is hidden (an idea most beautifully illustrated by the yin and yang symbol). If we identify as weak, when we really look we'll inevitably find strength or some similar quality. Our endless void transforms into a fountain of fullness. We discover that our sense of lack contains all that we desired.

Despite the appearance of opposites, and our identification with one over another, we find that really we're part of an indivisible whole. We come back to the source and are re-sourced. We discover rich resources right where we least expected to find them, in the darkest, most deficient and painful places.

On Defending and Resisting

One Sunday in my mid-twenties, I went to a family dinner with my boyfriend at the time. His mother, usually a model of English middle-class decorum, unexpectedly got drunk and embarked on an alcohol-fueled honesty spree, to everyone's embarrassment. When it came to my turn, she was mercifully brief: "You, Fiona Robertson. You only let people in so far and then the portcullis comes down." *In vino veritas,* I thought. I knew that portcullis, the metaphorical iron gate which defended my personal castle, only too well—even though I'd never named it before. The description was so apt because a portcullis is the last line of defense during an attack or siege.

Two or three years later, the sudden death of a close friend triggered a time of profound change. It was as if that heavy, iron grille slowly raised, partway at least, and out came grief, shame, rage, fear, and creativity—all repressed since childhood. I finally mourned for the loss of my best friend a decade earlier, for my father's absence, for the years that I'd spent battling food and body-image demons.

While I realized the catharsis was healing, I also spent a lot of energy trying not to feel the pain. Sex, cigarette smoking, meditation, and a plethora of healing and self-help techniques weren't quite enough to stem the cathartic tide. Even so, the portcullis remained, particularly when it came to intimacy and relationships. I felt like the princess alone in the tower, with utterly impenetrable stone walls surrounding me.

Defensiveness and resistance have a bad reputation. We read that we're *supposed* to be accepting, allowing, open. We think we're *supposed* to be able to just let go. And when we can't—when we're holding on or desperately clinging, in denial, resisting with all our might—we feel that we've failed and judge ourselves for it. We're not the spiritual people we've aspired to be. We're even further away from awakening or enlightenment or peace than before. We're stuck, blocked, self-sabotaging, overcompensating. We seek ways to overcome or break down those recalcitrant parts of our psyche, trying to batter them into submission. We resist our resistance and defend against our defensiveness.

What we fail to see is that these supposedly unwelcome tendencies are there for good reason. At some point in our lives, nearly always when we were very young, we needed to protect or defend ourselves. Wounded at the core, in little bodies, and so vulnerable in every way, we came up with ingenious, amazing ways to stave off further harm. For some, that harm is obvious: beatings, loss, denigration, abuse, or neglect. For others it was subtler, the result of parental anxiety or control, or not feeling truly seen. Either way, the strategies that we devised so long ago to shield ourselves can't be given up easily. Back then, it felt like our survival depended on them; no wonder, then, that anxiety, fear, and terror emerge when we come close to that core wound.

In my experience as a Living Inquiries facilitator, I've seen over and over how resistance and defensiveness guard the deep pain of our core wound. As we get close, we encounter the portcullis, which manifests differently in everyone. Maybe the mind produces a flurry of thoughts, sleepiness comes on, or sensations of numbness or rigidity or irritation or hopelessness appear. We say things like, "I can't do this anymore" or "I want this to end" or "I can't focus" or "I want to hide" or "I can't let go." During an inquiry session, we let the resistance be exactly as it is, just as we let everything be as it is. No judgment. No attempts to avoid or assuage what's coming.

The "seeming self" consists of the words, images, and energies or sensations that appear to protect us. We look at the images of walls and portcullises and black holes and whatever else comes up. We meet that energy of defensiveness, letting it do whatever it needs to do. We notice that the space in which everything arises has no argument with any of it. As we stay with it all, inquiring into the protective layers that have accrued around the seeming self, we discover that it only gives us the *illusion* of protection.

Far from leaving us unprotected, the unraveling of the defended self naturally gives rise to healthier interpersonal boundaries. When the portcullis comes down, we have a clearer view of what's around us and our instincts are no longer obscured by resistance or rigid defensiveness. We find ourselves gauging people and situations with much more acuity, moving effortlessly away from or toward whatever is wrong or right for us in each moment.

What we discover when we let it all be, exactly as it is right here and now, is that our points of resistance and defense are actually keys to the inner sanctum. The energy of resistance and defense was only ever energy, with some thoughts and images attached. So when it is fully felt, it gives way and yields the precious, vulnerable, tender, delicate core that it was protecting. We encounter the beauty that lies beneath. Tears flow, our hearts melt. Openness, acceptance, and allowing simply happen. We realize our deep and perfect innocence in all this. And from that place, we stumble upon the glorious paradox: there is not a self to defend and there is nothing to resist.

On Examining the Evidence

An aphorism often used in the debate on matter versus spirit and loved by forensic scientists is, "Just because you can't see it doesn't mean it's not there."

We rarely question the evidence upon which our assumptions are built, particularly when it comes to what we believe about ourselves, others, and the world. "Evidence" is defined in the dictionary* as "an appearance from which inferences may be drawn; the ground for belief." It comes from the Latin *ex* (out of, from within) and *videre* (to see, to perceive, to notice). With evidence, we trust that our senses are giving us reliable information we can use to draw conclusions about reality. Perceiving is believing. And in some areas of life that approach works.

We think we know how things are. "Of course she didn't love me." "It's obvious that they are hateful and ignorant." "It's clear that I'm a failure." And we keep a mental locker full of evidence to support these assertions. Thoughts, memories, and emotions seem to back up our story. We're reluctant to admit, or may not even realize, that our memories are selective. We edit, delete, and distort our recollections so that our alibis stand up to scrutiny.

For years, I told a story about the sweater that my mother started knitting me as a present for my eighth birthday. It wasn't finished in time, so she gave it to me for Christmas, ten months later. When I finally tried it on, it was too small. I took it as further evidence, as if any more was required, that I was her least favorite, the one who didn't matter. Recently, it came up in conversation and we laughed about it. Then my mother said, "But you remember the other sweater

---

* *Online Etymology Dictionary*, s.v. "evidence," accessed May 3, 2016, http://www.etymonline.com/index.php?term=evidence.

I knitted you, don't you? The grey one that you loved." I was jolted by the memory, realizing that I'd forgotten all about it. It hadn't fit with my version of events, my notion of me as "the one who got left out."

As a Living Inquiries facilitator, I've spent many hours with others closely examining the evidence that seems to back up our beliefs that include, "I don't belong," "I can't commit," "I shouldn't need," "I'll do it wrong, no matter what," "I'm not enlightened," "I'm not good enough," "I'm insatiably needy." This evidence is deeply felt and it seems utterly real and incontrovertible. We look at the locker, full of evidence and often sealed shut for many years, and we take out each item, one by one. Words. Images. Sensations. Emotions. Not trying to prove or disprove, rationalize or debate; not trying to negate or deny or shun. Just looking, feeling, being with whatever's there, in whatever form it comes.

After a while, it inevitably becomes clear that the objects we're looking at—sometimes very painful, other times funny, often shockingly and wonderfully random—can't possibly be taken as proof of anything. The identity that we've believed in so completely begins to fall apart as the flimsy, insubstantial nature of the evidence is revealed. Half-remembered fragments, vague or vivid images, energy in the body, powerful or subtle emotion—none of it adds up to a coherent whole.

We've often spent years trying to hide, bury, or run away from the evidence, and yet, when we really look and examine it forensically, it becomes apparent that it is totally benign. We are guilty of nothing. There's no charge to answer. We are utter innocence.

As paradoxical as it may seem, we discover that the presence of evidence isn't evidence of presence, any more than the absence of evidence is evidence of absence. During the lovingly rigorous inquiry process, we leave no stone unturned. Everything is held up to the light and recognized for what it is. Inevitably, we see that what we truly are is way beyond any evidence or belief. And at that point, the struggle ends.

On Excluding Nothing

There is no right answer to inquiry. There is no punch line, no state to reach, no necessary outcome. We start where we start and end up where we end up. There's no manipulation of experience, no preference for one feeling over another, no judgment of what appears. We don't attempt to understand, rationalize, analyze, or explain. We're simply here, with whatever shows up in the moment.

There is such simple relief found by allowing it all to *be*, by being allowed to let it all be. One of the joys of facilitating the Living Inquiries is to sit with someone in love, fear, hate, sadness, joy, peace, grief, jealousy, envy, distraction, frustration, rage, shame, anger, terror, boredom, indifference, love, loneliness, happiness, or any other shade of emotion…and do nothing. No commentary. No sympathy. No cajoling. No teaching or advising. No fixing of any kind. We humans have a tendency to believe that nothing will get done unless we do it, that nothing can be solved or changed without effort, acts of will, or struggle. Yet when we step aside, even for a moment, change happens. Life flows. Transformation occurs.

It can be a challenge to open the door to it all and say yes to whatever comes. Most of us have spent a lifetime attempting to regulate our feelings; like vigilant gatekeepers, we've tried so hard to feel the things we think we should be feeling and shut out the rest. So when we sit down to inquire, alone or with each other, it's natural for there to be some apprehension. We're taking a step into the unknown, into previously uncharted territory.

Finally, everything that has been denied can come in from the cold.

By staying with whatever is here, in whatever guise it appears—inquiring as we go—an unraveling happens. What we previously took to be real and incontrovertible becomes translucent, ephemeral. The deepest suffering and the most magnificent pleasures are found to be equally mysterious. There is such a delightful alchemy that arises when we meet each other, here and now, and directly look—excluding nothing. Love, fear, hate, tears: we can welcome whatever you bring.

On Fully Feeling What We're Not

We take ourselves to be the person who our thoughts tell us that we are. The coexistence of thoughts, images, emotions, and sensations creates a compelling and seemingly incontrovertible experience of *me*. And if that experience is painful or difficult—which is often the case—we spend a great deal of time and energy attempting to move away from it, in all kinds of subtle and not-so-subtle ways.

We each wear many labels that are made out of our thoughts, which we use to assemble our identity. Every label has its own tone, its own unique content. Some labels we wear proudly, making sure they're on public display as often as possible. Others, we ashamedly keep hidden, fearing exposure. A few are so repellent, so unbearable, that we relegate them to the shadows, ensuring that even we can't see them. Whether we see ourselves as deeply flawed works in progress, or as the perfectly satisfactory finished article, there's a sense of needing to hold up and maintain the structure. When someone contradicts, challenges, or confirms our labels, we react. We're hurt, angry, offended, pleased, or defensive. Conflict arises and we struggle. It all feels very real; what we think, imagine, feel, and sense seem to provide all the evidence we need that things are the way they appear to be.

Our identities are a carefully choreographed dance: protecting and defending, evading and avoiding. Sometimes the dance is on a public stage, sometimes it's a private performance. Rarely do we ever take a peek backstage or behind the scenes to examine the assumptions we live by. Instead, we do our best to mitigate the discomfort or suffering we feel, whether it's slight or intense.

As if our existence depended on it (which, on one level, it does), we find myriad ways to keep ourselves from fully feeling what lies at the core of each label. We're all familiar with unhealthy forms of

self-medication like alcohol, drugs, loveless sex, and endless television. But supposedly more positive activities, such as meditation,
therapy, sport, or spiritual practice can also be used in the same
self-medicating way. Underneath it all, we are full of dread that the
edifice of "me" will one day come crashing down, so we do everything in our power to stop that from happening, as much as we
simultaneously long for it. However, it is the refusal to be with what
seem to be our deepest truths that perpetuates them. As Sandra
Maitri says, "Paradoxically, at least to the mind, the more we
immerse ourselves in our experience, the more we become disiden-
tified with it."*

When we finally cease analyzing, strategizing, controlling,
avoiding, and defending the fake me that we have assembled—even
for a short while—we get to discover what the label has been cover-
ing up.

During the past few years, I've spent many hours each week
facilitating journeys in the Living Inquiries. Just as crucially, I've
been fortunate to have others who have facilitated my own inquiries. I've seen how, when we start to look into each identity, its true
contents are revealed. We've opened boxes labeled "I'm bad," "I'm
clever," "I'm not good enough," "I'm broken," "I'm the one that
can't," "I'm a failure," "I'm alone," "I'm the one who doesn't want to
be me," as well as so many more, and found that each box contains
words (thoughts), pictures (memories and imaginings), sensations in
the body, and emotions. We've looked carefully at each item and
allowed the sensations and emotions to be there, exactly as they are.
Often, we feel emotions that have never been truly felt before: the
raw, searing pain of grief; the raging energy of anger; the fragile,
delicate pull of longing. No running, no hiding, no justifying, no
mitigating, no making sense of it.

In that open space of looking, it gradually dawns that those col-
lections do not, in fact, make up a solid identity. A few words here,

---

* Sandra Maitri, *The Spiritual Dimension of the Enneagram* (New York: Penguin
Books, 2001).

a sequence of images there, some tingling, a little contraction, a flood of tears…and that's all. There is no one who is unlovable, bad, clever, alone, or anything else. Ultimately, we can't find the one that we've taken ourselves to be. It is only by having the courage to open those boxes with their labels (even the ones that are surrounded with barbed wire, armed guards, and "keep out" signs) that we're able to discover the deeper truth of who we are. By fully feeling what we're not, our hearts break open to the freedom beyond.

Are you willing to look?

On Guarding Against Love

Your task is not to seek for love, but merely to seek and find all the barriers within yourself that you have built against it.*

Many of our stories revolve around love and the having, or not having, of it. "She loves me." "She doesn't love me." "I'm unlovable." "I'm loving." We seek it out, talk about it, lament its loss, and celebrate its gain. What we often fail to notice is that, despite our protestation to the contrary, we've also fortified ourselves against it. With good reason, for the love that we're all really seeking is the end of separation, and that means the end of the person who we've taken ourselves to be.

An effortless love arises between us when we meet without our deficiency stories. Whoever we are, whatever our background or biographies, we recognize ourselves in each other; we know that we are one. Finally, we get what we've longed for: to be truly seen.

Wonderful as that is, it's also threatening to the separate, deficient self, as I experienced recently when a friend's sweet remark gave rise to inexplicable anxiety. After a disturbed night, feeling like I'd returned to a painfully familiar place, I met with a fellow facilitator to take a look. Using the Anxiety Inquiry, we looked for the attack and the one who is under attack. What arose were: images (the Facebook screen, my mother, my father, fragments of a dream); words ("I'm only safe when I don't take up space," "I've tried so hard to not be me"); sensations (contractions in the chest and solar

---

* The author of these lines is uncertain. While widely attributed to Rumi, it is also found in *A Course in Miracles* by Helen Schucman and William Thetford.

plexus, the energies of defense and keeping things out); emotions (fear and sadness). Each moment taken, allowed to be, looked at. None of them an attack, none of them the one under attack.

Then came stuckness from feelings of holding on and not being safe without protection. We stayed with the energy, letting it be just as it was. "Yes, that's me, the one who is under attack." After a while, an image arose of a caterpillar, struggling to emerge from its cocoon. "I don't want to be her anymore." The sense of attack remained. At that moment, the facilitator asked me:

"What's the worst that could happen?"

My answer was that I could be loved.

"What's the worst that could happen if you were loved?"

I could lose *me*.

"And if you lost you, then what would happen?"

It would be blissful. I was suddenly awash with relief.

When we looked again for the attack, all I could find was attacking energy moving outward. Images of movement in nature came up: fish swimming, flowers opening, branches moving in the wind. And suddenly, it hit me. "I'm not a mistake, I'm supposed to be like this. All this time, I've been trying to not be a mistake, in the belief that I was." No attack, no one under attack, just a simple and innocent misperception.

As my wise friend said later, "Funny, looking back at that brief exchange you wouldn't think it could tap into something so deep. And yet, in doing so, it unraveled into something quite wonderful." There are no mistakes, however much we feel there are. Everything is love, calling to us. Everything—every interaction, every sensation, every emotion, every thought—is an invitation to love, into seeing that we have never been separate.

On Having One Regret

A friend of mine once told me that she had only one regret: a few months previously, she bought a pair of pants but not the matching jacket. I was stunned. Even a little appalled. Was that it? Was there really nothing else in her life that she regretted? I felt suspicious about what was behind her lack of regret, not sure whether to attribute it to a charmed life, superficiality, or a complete acceptance of life as it is. But I couldn't believe that any one of those possibilities was actually the case.

At the time, I had mounds of regrets. I wished that I'd studied harder and done more at university. I felt as if I'd passed up useful opportunities which might never come my way again. I felt bad about sleeping with as many boyfriends as I had. I would, on occasion, lie awake at night, mulling over each relationship and detailing the reasons why it had been a mistake. I berated myself for smoking, drinking, and not being more in shape. I found it nearly impossible to forgive myself for some of my choices: the mundane and insignificant as well as the major and life-changing.

Being a perfectionist didn't help. I was bound to fail to live up to the ideal image that I carried around in my head. The messiness of life and the complexity of human interactions consistently foiled my effort to make life work in the way that I thought it should. Constantly sensing a gap between what was and what should be, it was difficult to let go of the notion that I had somehow got it all dreadfully wrong.

It is only when we start to closely examine our stories that we begin to see the assumptions that underpin our regrets. Regret says, "I know what should have happened and it wasn't that." Regret says, "I'm in control of life." Regret says, "I'm responsible for all the choices that I've made." Regret believes that it's up to us to determine how our lives turn out, so it's our fault if things aren't going well. Regret pretends that it knows what's best, which is nothing more than fantasy and the story of self-blame. "I did wrong and I should have done right."

I slowly began to dismantle the foundations of the House of Regret. I realized that there was no way I could possibly know what should have happened. That I'm not in control of life. That I don't know what's best and that there is no right or wrong outside of thought. I stopped believing in the past as some kind of fixed entity, as a place that I'd inhabited and could revisit. The subtle notion that past actions or events could somehow be transmuted by regret ceased to make any sense. I realized that regret keeps the past alive but semicomatose and it keeps us bound in a dead narrative that prevents us from fully feeling the aliveness of painful emotions.

After a while, memories no longer stirred such uncomfortable emotions and forgiveness gradually came. Now, I no longer lie awake at night plagued by regrets about boyfriends, things I have said or done, and things I have not said or not done. Now, I think it was okay that I spent my time at university going to music gigs and smoking dope—I'm even a little impressed that I still managed to churn out some decent essays and earn a degree.

When regret does appear, it doesn't last long, as I'm able to question its very basis. I can watch as the story of me, of what I should or shouldn't have done, ebbs and flows.

I have held on to one last, long-standing regret. When I was nineteen, I returned home during the holidays to clear out my old room. In two plastic bags were all the letters I'd ever been sent and the diaries that I'd written in every day for seven years, between the ages of eleven and eighteen. My older sister chided me for keeping them and I put them in the trash. The next morning, I regretted my decision but it was too late. The garbage had already been collected. By keeping the regret, it's as if I get to keep the letters and diaries. And I'm not quite ready to give them up, just yet.

On Having the Courage to Look

The Living Inquiries are not for halfhearted dabblers. If you simply want to feel more comfortable, improve your life, reach a state of permanent contentment, or otherwise become a better you, I'd advise you to step away now. Really. Because once you let the cat out of the bag, it's unlikely you'll ever be able to stuff it back in again. This kind of looking leaves no stone unturned, and it takes courage.

When we talk about ourselves and our lives, we inevitably and usually unconsciously edit or shape the content to reflect what we believe to be true. If our basic sense of ourselves is that we're a victim, we filter out anything that suggests otherwise. If we feel that we're unlovable, the stories we tell reflect that. By doing this, even though the identity that we've espoused is inevitably painful, we defend and nurture it. It's familiar, if uncomfortable. It feels like who we actually are, so we don't realize that we can question its very basis.

Whatever our stories are, deep wounds are at their cores, and we spend our lives doing everything we can to avoid or numb the pain. We find all kinds of ingenious ways to evade the wounds, even as they inform our every move and permeate our relationships with others and the world at every turn. We'll do anything rather than simply feel the pain, from spiritual practices and questing for enlightenment to taking drugs or bingeing on television.

The Inquiries offer us the opportunity to do just that—to simply feel it.

As many of us are discovering, simply staying with, and looking directly at, whatever comes—with no added interpretation, theorizing, analysis, understanding, judgment, commentary, or sympathy—

is an astonishingly powerful and transformative process. This is particularly the case when we meet with a facilitator. We find ourselves in a place of raw, searing honesty as we share each word and every image, exactly as it appears. Sentences that we have barely breathed to ourselves are finally uttered to another to be witnessed and held for the first time. Buried memories resurface; images of all kinds arise to be seen. Sensations and emotions emerge as an ever-changing flow of energy in the body. All of it is, at last, unscripted, unedited, uncensored, unexpurgated.

As the present-moment looking continues, we have no idea what will come next. If we've been used to trying to control our experience, this can be unsettling. Our carefully crafted identity begins to be seen as the illusion it is, and we touch the wounds that we've been holding at bay. All our strategies and sidesteps crumble. Sometimes that's breathtakingly painful and at other times it's hysterically funny. Either way, it takes courage to step beyond the familiar and into the territory of the unknown. We need bravery to feel what we've spent a lifetime avoiding.

As many have said before, there's no endpoint on sale here. No promises of any kind. But if you're willing to look, we're here to look with you. If you're willing to examine all your notions of who, how, where or what you are or should be, you've come to the right place.

Oh, and as it turns out, even the wounds are ultimately unfindable.

On Honoring Our Stories

The stories we tell about ourselves and our lives get a bad rap in some circles. We're exhorted to look past them, to see them as "just" stories and to transcend them. We may even end up feeling bad for having them in the first place, as if it were possible not to have them, which adds more layers to each story because we are denigrating it and ourselves for stupidity, weakness, or whatever other faults or wrongness we ascribe to ourselves.

Here's another view: rather than a hurdle to be overcome, pushed aside, or seen through, each story is an invitation to look more deeply. Whatever it happens to be in the moment, a long-running saga or a freshly conceived belief, it can be honored.

I've spent more than twenty years listening to people's stories—the mundane, the horrifying, the heartrending, and everything in between—in a variety of settings. When the story is given its due, listened to with care and attention, and honored simply for being, inevitably it opens up to yield yet more of itself. On being acknowledged—not agreed, colluded, or sympathized with, but wholeheartedly received and accepted—there's a movement deeper within.

For example, we may begin by telling our story of how badly someone has behaved toward us: "I can't believe she said that to me. How dare she?" When we (as either storyteller or listener) let the story be just as it is, without trying to edit, rationalize, or curtail it in any way, very soon we find ourselves in the deeper story, whatever that may be. "I'm so hurt." "I feel abandoned." "I'm scared."

Our stories don't arise randomly or by accident. We make them up for a reason and they are not solely a product of the ego, that part of our psyche which analyzes, judges, and sustains the separate "I." Over the years, we are deeply affected by events in our lives; that's not a fault, it's simply what it is to be human. Sometimes, we find ourselves telling the same stories over and over again, probably because there's something in them that we haven't yet fully connected with. Perhaps a feeling or a deeper, unconscious belief wants to be heard or seen. We may have stories that we have never told anyone else, maybe because we can't countenance them ourselves or because they bring up shame, grief, fear, or some other seemingly intolerable emotion. Either way, telling the story is vital if we are to heal. For all the elements of the story—the narrative itself as well as the accompanying images, memories, feelings, emotions, and sensations—to be heard, seen, and felt, we simply need to be willing to hear, see, and feel, without judgment or criticism or self-attack.

When it doesn't feel possible to do that for ourselves, we can turn to one another. Something I love about the Living Inquiries community is that we *all* tell our stories and are willing to inquire into them; we are all willing to tell our truth as it seems to be in that moment. The open, safe, nonjudgmental space that is held by the facilitator in sessions allows us to tell even the most disturbing or horrific of our stories.

In each session, we begin with the story that's uppermost. Usually there's a narrative to it, although it may even arise without words, simply a sensation or energy in the body. Not only do we allow and open to the story, we look at it closely, often word by word, letting the body respond to it just as it does. As we do this, more layers or aspects of the story begin to reveal themselves: a childhood memory, a familiar feeling of humiliation, or more words.

I sometimes use an analogy to describe what we do during sessions. It's as if there's a pile of boxes or baggage in the corner of the room, which we normally try to ignore even though we have to maneuver around it all the time because it's in the way. Each box has a label on it: "I'm useless" or "Fear of loss" or "I want chocolate." When we are finally willing to turn to a box and open it up, we find a collection of words, images, and feelings inside it. As we take out each element and either look at it or feel it, that leads us to the next

On Investigating the Obvious

One day, when I was about eight years old, my mother and I were in the local produce store. I waited and listened as she chatted with a neighbor. As I heard the words, "And how is your other son?" I realized that the woman had made a terrible mistake. There was only one boy in our family, my older brother. She thought I was a boy. Horrified and indignant, I spoke up loudly: "I'm a girl!"

Gender is absolutely central to how we identify ourselves. Along with ethnicity, cultural background, nationality, and sexual preference, it usually feels fixed and immutable. Whatever else we see ourselves as—unlovable, competent, not good enough, peaceful, angry—the basic facts of our bodies appear to speak for themselves. Female, male, white, black, English, Indian, gay, straight, whatever we happen to be, it seems we cannot help but relate to the world through the prism of our form.

During my twenties, I strongly identified as a feminist. I worked my way through Shulamith Firestone's *The Dialectic of Sex*. I played in an all-female band (I bet no one ever asked John, Paul, George, or Ringo why they didn't have women in the group) and centered my social life around a community of like-minded women, some of whom were separatist feminist lesbians. I occasionally cursed my stubborn heterosexuality for not allowing me to disengage from men altogether, believing that I would be better off without them. I was alert for all forms of prejudice or oppression, particularly sexism, racism, and homophobia. A long list of "isms" and "anti-isms" seemed to define me. Eventually, my opinions softened a little through the arrival of motherhood, a growing interest in self-development and spirituality, and a change in the prevailing mood. These changes all shifted my focus from the political to the personal.

I've been wondering what happens when we inquire into something that seems to be objectively true. Is there any value to looking into the obvious? As everyone who has encountered the Living Inquiries knows, we generally look at the things that seem to cause us suffering, such as negative self-beliefs, cravings, addiction, conflict in relationships, sadness, anger, anxiety, or fear. I wasn't aware that I felt any particular suffering around being a woman, but was curious to see what may be revealed by investigating more deeply. So I recently took a look, with the help of another facilitator.

"I'm a woman."

"Are you those words?"

What unfolded as the inquiry progressed was beyond anything I could have imagined. There were archetypal images: Neolithic goddesses with pronounced breasts and bellies and Eve in the Garden of Eden. This was followed by memories of menarche and the shame and humiliation that came along with bleeding. It emerged that I'd felt betrayed by my body, that I'd grieved for the freedom of prepubescence, that I'd believed I had to stop being myself. I journeyed through birth and breastfeeding, sex and feminine power. I raged at the way patriarchy has made women's experiences taboo and then saw my deep-rooted belief that being a woman meant suffering.

As we stayed with the various physical sensations, it became clear that I've held my body in particular ways, as if trying to force myself into this shape. Laughter came, along with the words, "We make a whole identity out of a bunch of sensations." It also became clear that this body—however much I've both judged it and identified with it—isn't who I truly am. As the pattern of holding relaxed, I felt a merging of masculine and feminine energy; the words "alchemical marriage" appeared. "I'm no different from men." A sense of expansion followed, a taking up of more space. I keenly felt the pain of definition, the pain that ensues every time we define ourselves as *this* and *not that*.

Most powerfully of all, I saw how we suffer because we label each other. Suddenly overwhelmed with sadness at the violence our labeling causes, I saw how I've labeled myself. I saw my belief that being a girl is second best and the effort I've put into proving that I'm not second best. In that moment, I realized the utter uniqueness of us all, the absolute impossibility of comparison.

This inquiry continues to unfold within me. There's a subtle sense of moving in the world less apologetically. I feel more earthed, more rooted in my body. As ever, I'm deeply humbled at the power of these Inquiries. Every time we look, more is revealed, and yet we find less. The less we find, the fuller life gets. This is truly paradoxical and absolutely breathtaking.

On Naming

Our night, at dinner, we talked about our children. One friend described how her toddler, currently in the question phase, incessantly asks, "What's that name?" Any sound he hears and anything he sees evokes the same question. She does her best to give him an answer: "It's a man down the road, doing 'Bob the Builder,' mending his house." He's gathering language and discovering the world of concepts. Usually he's satisfied with her explanations but sometimes he persists: "No, Mommy—what's that name?" Occasionally, exhausted, she abandons her attempts to describe and makes something up like, "That's Steve."

Our ability to name things gives us a sense of control. Whether it's external objects—birds, trees, planets, makes of cars, other people—or internal objects like sensations, we feel a greater dominion over things that we are able to name. "I've given it a name, so now I understand it." Like Adam in the Garden of Eden, we believe that things are what we call them. What we don't fully appreciate—until we really look—is that the activity of naming often keeps us one step removed and reinforces our sense of separateness.

Nowhere is this more apparent than in the emotional realm. It seems that talking about our feelings, however articulately, can be another way to resist actually feeling them. In fact, it is a way to solidify, and even sanctify, what we're feeling. In our rush to name the feeling "fear," "shame," "love," "guilt," "happiness," "sadness," or "anger," we objectify it and then feel obliged to relate as if it's somehow separate from us. As if it is ours to hold onto, get rid of, or deal with. Subject and object.

To fully immerse ourselves in the raw experience of emotion demands that we give up our conceptualizing. All of it. The Living

Inquiries are an exceptionally effective way to deconstruct an emotion. By breaking it down into its constituent parts of words, images, and sensations in the body, and then looking closely at each part, we come to see that the emotion is not what we've assumed it to be. Over and over, we find that our assumptions do not stand up to scrutiny. Because, for example, it turns out that what we've believed to be "guilt" is actually a word, plus a couple of images that arise, plus a sensation of contraction in the solar plexus. Without the word and the images, the sensation is just that—a physical sensation. It has no inherent meaning. It's not saying anything. Allowed to just be, without explanation or interpretation or even description, it is fully felt and it inevitably dissipates.

This activity of un-naming leaves us in the quiet spaciousness of not knowing. When we are able to see words without the heavy weight of associations, we lighten up. A few months ago, with one of the other facilitators, I looked for myself, for "Fiona," using the Unfindable Inquiry process. I was astounded by the feelings of responsibility that came up, as I believed that I had to make The Fiona Project a success. When the things we've named prove to be unfindable, over and over again, it seems we experience stillness more often. Nothing to hold onto. No place to land.

A paradoxical delight then emerges. We see that things don't exist outside of thought, image, sensation, and emotion—yet we're even more fully engaged with life. We enjoy talking, describing, and discussing, even as we know that our ideas and opinions are not us. We continue to entertain each other with our stories, only our plot twists, characters, and narrative arcs are taken less seriously. We continue to name things. Like dogs bark and cats meow, it's just what we do.

What's in a name? that which we call a rose
By any other name would smell as sweet.
      —William Shakespeare, *Romeo and Juliet*

On Resting

One January morning, I awoke in pain and by the next day had undergone emergency surgery for a rare ovarian condition. The day after I was operated on, a large retaining wall behind my house collapsed, damaging the garden and rendering the central heating system useless. After nearly a week in the hospital, I returned home to spend the rest of the month convalescing next to a portable gas heater, surrounded by piles of sleeping bags.

At the time, I was a community development worker, based in a particularly deprived area of the city. Young and politically motivated, I believed that we were making a difference and that my presence was, in some minor way, changing the world. I was also conscientious, so it was a challenge to be off work for so long. For a while, I was too ill to be concerned about what was happening in my absence. But as the month wore on, I began to wonder and to fret about all that I supposed wasn't getting done and all those meetings that I hadn't been able to attend.

When I eventually returned to work, the shocking truth was that everything had carried on perfectly well without me. My absence really hadn't made much of a difference. My colleagues said they'd missed me and there was some work to catch up on, but it became very clear that I was dispensable. I'd subtly believed myself to be indispensable—then life showed me that this was far from the case. Nothing had fallen apart in my absence, with the exception of the retaining wall, and I could hardly take credit for that.

Over the next few months, I slowly got better and the wall and the heating were eventually repaired. For a while, I remembered the lesson: it is okay to take time off, life does not require my continuous activity. Since then, however, I've fallen into the same trap several times, believing myself to be indispensable and not taking a rest even when I needed one. Inevitably, life has intervened and the break has come anyway, often not of my own choosing.

This experience is not just personal; it is also cultural. We've become more averse to stopping and resting. Now that we're constantly connected, our physical absence makes little difference and it's even more tempting to just keep on keeping on, wherever we are. "What I do is so important that I can't really take a break." The credo seems to be, "I'm busy, therefore I'm important." Even commerce no longer takes time off; at least the old English Sunday trading laws—which ruled that all but the smallest shops had to be shut—reminded us that we were supposed to be having a day of rest. But those have long since been revised.

It seems that our identities are so bound up with what we do, with our busyness, that we find it unsettling, if not frightening, to really stop and rest. We like to believe that there are things out there that need to be done and that we shouldn't put down our tools until they are done. We believe that things only get done because we exert our will and that it is our pushing or forcing our activity that makes things happen. We are pleased with ourselves when we feel that we have achieved something, been constructive, and crossed tasks off our list.

All this activity distracts us from our deeper feelings, from the intractable questions that inevitably surface during the quieter times. "Do I make any difference?" "Is there any meaning to life?" "What happens when we die?"

A couple of years ago, I began to experiment with doing nothing for an hour or so at a time. Not meditating, not doing, no agenda other than no agenda. Just sitting, or lying, and seeing what happened. Sometimes, I'd cry. Sometimes, I'd lie on the floor with my legs against the wall or I'd move around like young children do, aimlessly and entirely without purpose. At times, I'd be moved to write, or look at old photos, or read a passage from a particular book. My rigid sense of self loosened a little further each time and I began to see through my belief that not being engaged in purposeful activity meant that I was lazy, or a little crazy, or both. Being a grown up came to seem less onerous, less serious.

Recently, I've felt the need to stop again after going through an exhausting time. It has been tempting to believe the train of thought that says, "There is so much to do! You can't stop yet. You need to sort out the house and earn a steady income." And for a while, I was caught up in those thoughts. But when I remembered that I can stop to rest and everything will be fine, I resolved to do as little as possible for a week. As long as I feed the three of us—the dog, the fish, and me—all will be well.

On Separating Fact from Fantasy

When I was very young, I had three invisible friends. One of them was a Manx cat with no tail. I'd insist that seats were left for them at the dinner table and I'd kiss them goodnight. For a time, they were as real to me as my brother and sisters, and far less troublesome. Naturally, as I got older, they faded from my world. I grew up, or so I thought.

As little children, we attempt to make sense of the world around us. We become aware that we're a somebody and that there are other somebodies around us. We scrabble around for an identity, trying to work out who we are. We naturally and innocently gather information from observing other people's behaviors and responses, and we become increasingly aware of our internal experience—our own thoughts and feelings. Our sense of ourselves—the sense of *me*—is molded from a motley collection of things we've been told, beliefs, and physical sensations, taken as a whole. In the early years, it seems to have some permeability, some fluidity, but over time it becomes more solid, more set—until we have a definite sense of *me* and *who I am*.

As adults, we like to believe that we know what's going on and that we're objective, logical, and reasonable. We've collectively placed a premium on fact, yet we're largely blind to the fact that much of what we take to be true is actually fantasy. All of our ideas about ourselves and others *feel* true, so we believe them. My thoughts and feelings tell me that I'm no good, or wrong, or worthless (there are many variants) and my experiences seem to prove that I'm right. So I become firmly convinced that I am, in fact, the person who is no good, or wrong, or worthless. And I go about life acting as if that were the case, very rarely stopping to question the validity of my assumption.

Something similar happens in other areas of our experience. We believe that we're right about other people and that our estimation of who they are is factually correct. While we may well acknowledge that our fears are irrational, or that our addictions are unreasonable, we appear relatively powerless in the face of them because they don't yield to logic or reason, however hard we try to justify them. Again, our fears *feel* very real, and our addictions are fueled by a compelling combination of thoughts and physical cravings.

As a result, in most areas of our lives, we live in a fantasy of *as if*. We live as if the world is unsafe, or as if other people don't like us, or as if we have to drink alcohol or eat cake to survive. We live as if we're inadequate or damaged or not enough. Simply because we've assumed that what we believe is true. Convinced that we're grown up, and therefore know how things are, we're actually trying to navigate through life with an outmoded belief structure that hasn't substantially changed since we were young children.

Not surprisingly, we tend to resist really looking at our fundamental beliefs about ourselves, others, and the world. As we look, it can feel as if we're in real danger; we assume that because this structure has protected us, it is necessary to our survival. The fear of *not being this* often emerges during Living Inquiry sessions. "If I'm not this, then what am I? Without this, I'll be annihilated." We end up trying to defend or hold onto the very things that seem to cause us the most suffering because it feels safer to do so. Better the devil you know.

The good news is that it takes very little looking, relatively speaking, to begin loosening these fantastical beliefs—this mishmash of thoughts, images, sensations, and emotions that we've taken to be reality. It constantly amazes me that core beliefs, things that we've taken ourselves or the world to be on the deepest levels, can be unraveled in an hour or two.

I'll share a personal example: I firmly believed that I was irretrievably damaged. I wasn't even aware of believing it, it simply seemed to be the case and was backed up by plenty of evidence. All my life, I'd acted as if that's what I were. As I worked with a fellow facilitator one day, the belief itself came to light at the beginning of the session. As we looked for me, the person who is irretrievably damaged, all kinds of thoughts came up, along with images and memories, and a host of powerful sensations and emotions, including shame. I sobbed. We continued looking, and after an hour and a half, the one who is irretrievably damaged was nowhere to be found. The complete innocence of that belief also became startlingly apparent. It was simply a mistake, a childish and totally blameless misinterpretation of information.

What happens when we see through these beliefs, when we see that our ideas are as insubstantial as my invisible friends? Over time, a subtle change occurs. The childish reactivity that we tend to display when we feel deficient or threatened starts to quiet. In its place comes a steadiness, a greater equilibrium. We no longer know what's going on or who we are, which feels so much more solid, so much more mature. Life's dramas become less intense and less serious. Living life as it is, rather than living life *as if*, turns out to be much more interesting than we could have imagined. In fact, it's fantastic.

On Taking the Last Stand

As we inquire into our most deeply held notions about who we are—our core deficiency stories—we often encounter the fear of moving beyond them. We may even encounter terror, as if we're at the threshold of an abyss or a void. These identities have been our refuge, after all. They are painful, but they are what we know. And so we hold onto them, grabbing, grasping, and petrified of what may come next. "If that's not me, then what is? My whole life will be taken away from me. What would I be without this?" It's as if we'll lose everything, both ourselves and our lives, if we step across that threshold. We're not going to go down without a fight.

Some days, my deficiency stories are at the helm. When my all-time, number-two story—*I'm under attack*—is at the forefront, I feel shaky, sensitive to criticism, and anxious. I don't sleep well. I become shy and awkward around men and I can feel shunned by women.

During one particular episode of this, even a very well-facilitated inquiry session didn't make a difference. For the first time ever, I found the self I was looking for. She was right there, still under attack, resolutely dug into the trenches and refusing to move.

When I came to inquire again, still very much in the same state, it became clear that my number-one deficiency story—*I'm not wanted*—lay just beneath the feeling of being attacked. As my fellow facilitator took me into the heart of the story, my defenses held. "This is who I am. I don't know what else to be. I am the one who is unwanted. Always have been. Always will be. That's just the way it is."

Then the words "Custer's Last Stand" appeared in my mind and I knew it was game over. Finally, I discovered why I've battled so long and hard when an image of a little girl appeared, an inner me that I had to protect. "I've looked after her for so long. I'm not giving her up." As we stayed with the image, the realizations came:

I thought there was a little girl here.

I thought there was a big girl here, come to that.

I thought somebody was trying to take something away.

It's all been a story.

It's all been a story I've never had any choice in.

I thought it was all my fault.

I thought I was unwanted because there was something wrong with me.

Next came an image of a film set, the actors ready, the crew prepared, the director shouting, "Ready!"

I thought it was all real and there's something so sweet about that.

I've been a good little girl who has tried really, really hard to play her part well, even when it meant making things really difficult for myself.

There's been no choice and, simultaneously, I didn't understand there was a choice.

I've tried so hard to work it all out.

I didn't know it didn't need working out.

At this point, I saw an image of the late, great comedian Bill Hicks doing his "It's Just a Ride" piece. Then came the facilitator's question: "Who or what is aware of all that is transpiring right now?" The answer came to me immediately:

Life. The knowing or the awareness of it isn't any different
to it. It's everything being itself. This experience here isn't
separate from that. And it's also being itself, and being itself

is fine. There's nothing wrong with Fiona-ing. It's just all seeing itself.

From out of the tears and the intense sensations emerged a sense of excitement and fun. My mind evoked the film set again, the crew giving me and the other actors a round of applause, and the director saying, "Very good, everybody. Very good. Take five."

To which I replied, "Oh, you fuckers. I'm exhausted. I'm not taking a part like that again. Or maybe I am. We all get to dress up and do all this shit. How cool is that?"

How cool, indeed. The Living Inquiries are such a gift. Taking this intimate, experiential dive into what we've taken ourselves to be shows us that we never were that. Finally able to take our last stands, we realize that we've only ever been life. Which leaves me with awe, amazement, and gratitude.

All the world's a stage,
And all the men and women merely players

—William Shakespeare, As You Like It

On Telling It Like It Is

My old English dictionary, printed in 1932, is one of my favorite books. Bought many years ago from a secondhand bookstore, it badly needs rebinding. There are loose pages and some of the "M" words may have been lost forever. I've turned to it many times, usually to delve more deeply into the meaning of a word that particularly resonates within me. My journal is interspersed with dictionary definitions, written out alongside whatever I was recording at the time. This word-exploration has allowed me to drop even more deeply into whatever I am feeling at a given time and allowed the feeling to become even more itself. "Overwhelm." "Fault." "Blame." "Pathetic."

When we start to inquire, the first task is to determine accurately what we're inquiring into. As Scott says, "Name it." The more resonant the words we use to define what we're looking for are, the more likely that the looking will penetrate deeply. Sometimes we're looking for a very familiar self, an identity that we've been aware of forever. At other times, we don't consciously know what lies behind our current conflict, discomfort, or suffering. On those occasions, the Boomerang and Panorama Inquiries allow us to drop more deeply into our experience and to discover the senses of self that lies just out of reach. We know we've reached the right wording when we get the felt-sense of "Aha!", that perceptible sense of fit, often accompanied by emotion.

Naming it can be a challenge. What comes up in the moment may conflict with how we see ourselves, with our cherished views of who we are or how we're supposed to be. What comes up can be unflattering in the extreme. And that's the point. These are the places we haven't wanted to go to, the places that we've been avoiding, escaping, medicating, and running from. "I'm heartless." "I'm unwanted." "I'm failing." "I can't cope." Some of us have spent years attempting to polish the turd, undertaking therapy, medita- tion, spiritual practice, positive affirmations and the like—only to finally realize that nothing has really worked.

Then we come to the Living Inquiries and we're able to—at last—tell it like it is. And in that telling, we meet our deficiency stories head on, along with our resistance to those stories. We believe that we shouldn't be this way, that we shouldn't feel as we do. As we look at the words—these words that seem to contain our darkest, dirtiest secrets—we get to feel what makes them seem real. Emotions and sensations in the body become enmeshed with words and images, creating the sense that we are failing, or not coping, or unwanted. It is this "Velcro effect," as Scott calls it, that gives words their seeming power. The interlocking of words and images with sensations and emotions can make it feel as if we are the words, as if we're commanded or threatened by them.

As we unravel the tangle of self, the threads of deficiency that have kept us bound are picked apart. We see that we are not who we thought we were. This process of telling, which is an act of confes- sion, is powerful because when every word, image, sensation, and emotion is met just as it is—with no agenda to change, modify, judge, overcome, or repel it—it is finally set free. My dictionary gives a pertinent description of the word "confess": "To own; to acknowledge; to admit; to declare one's adhesion to a belief."* And that's really what we're doing as we inquire; we are declaring our beliefs and then examining them carefully. "I believe that I want the pain to stop." "I believe that I'm a person who is insignificant." "I believe I'm a person who is awakened." Through the simple act of telling it exactly lik it is, with no caveats, justifications, explana- tions, or pleas, we finally get to feel what has been there all along.

---

* *New English Dictionary*, ed. Ernest A. Baker (England and Wales: Odhams Press Ltd, 1932), s.v. "confess."

Leaving no stone unturned, every word uttered can be explored in this way. Any story that can be told can be inquired into, with the gentle, ruthless, compassionate insistence that characterizes the Living Inquiries. What has been hidden for so long is brought into the light, and seen for what it is.

On Thinking That We've Arrived
(or Not)

When I was a teenager, I yearned for the independence that being even a year or two older seemed to promise. I wanted to make my own decisions and act on them unimpeded by adult interventions. I vividly remember the desperate desire to leave home, to put away childish things. I wanted to be *there*, not stuck *here*.

The feeling that there is a destination to be reached, somewhere to get to, permeates our lives. Our societies are deeply aspirational; we're encouraged to want more, bigger, better. We carry around within us an impossible-to-achieve image of the ideal self, and then we set about trying to create that self. No matter whether our route to this idealized perfection is via slimming products, makeup, and haute couture—or affirmations, meditation, and yoga, the movement is the same. We're here and we want to be there.

In my thirties, I embarked on an intense search for healing. I spoke often of being "on the journey" and I loved that idea. I saw myself as a traveler, making my way courageously through difficult terrain, guided by intuition and the maps that my fellow travelers— those many miles further on—had created. It was very clear; there was a path and I was on it.

At the end of the journey, I knew I would find the Holy Grail: peace, clarity, wellness, and the end of suffering. I'd arrive home, at my final destination. Occasionally, I'd have the sense that I had made it. For a while, I'd feel calm, well, happy. Inevitably, before too long, I'd be off again, searching intently, longing to get there, to not be here with this—whatever this was.

I felt that I shouldn't be *here* in more mundane ways, too, particularly in relationships and social situations. Sometimes, it was possible to get up and leave, but on other occasions I was paralyzed, unable to move for fear or doubt. One boyfriend memorably said to me, "If you don't fucking like it, fuck off." Eventually, I did leave.

Over the years, I began to encounter spiritual concepts. Words like "oneness," "awakening," and "enlightenment" entered my vocabulary. Like nearly all spiritual seekers, I frequently fantasized about enlightenment. I imagined states of eternal bliss and transcendence, a complete absence of any kind of pain. Most of all, I imagined awakening as being completely other than this-here-now. It felt like there was distance—sometimes a yawning void—between here and there. *There* was the place that others talked about in books and videos. *There* was the Shangri-La I wanted to get to, the end of suffering, the place inhabited by the lucky few.

But how, exactly, was I supposed to get myself from here to there? I looked for instructions, prescriptions, suggestions, to no avail.

I would constantly monitor my experience for signs that I may be nearing the destination. "Ooh, I'm feeling incredibly calm and peaceful. Maybe this is it?" "Oh my god, I must be so far off if I'm like this, irritated and upset."

Like children on a road trip, the seeker's refrain seems to be, "Are we there yet?"

One day while walking my dog, I suddenly saw that there is only here. *There* does not exist. It is only ever a fleeing image, an idea that is happening here, just as everything else does. By conceptualizing enlightenment or happiness or peace as a state, or place, to be reached, and by objectifying it, we create a separation that doesn't actually exist. We place it outside ourselves, creating imaginary distance. We believe we have to find a way to bridge the gap, to get from here to there.

Recently, I looked for the self that shouldn't be *here*. Taken through the Unfindable Inquiry by one of my fellow facilitators, I touched on the pain that has been bound up in that lifelong story, and sobbed. Sweet release. I saw, yet again, how the story of separation is created by belief. It is not that we're in the wrong place. It is simply that there is nowhere else to go. We're here. That's it. We've arrived, whether we know it or not.

On Not Finding the Problem

Like many of us who find ourselves on a spiritual search, I spent many years trying to end my supposed suffering. I tried in all manner of ways, attempting to numb the pain with cigarettes, dope, sex, and relationship dramas. I embarked on quests for understanding, believing that counseling, psychotherapy, homeopathy, transpersonal psychology, or dream interpretation might hold the elusive key. I investigated an eclectic mix of healing modalities, from acupuncture and craniosacral therapy to hypnotherapy and nutrition. I ran the whole self-help gamut: I positively affirmed, meditated, journaled, and paid attention to my chakras. And there's no doubt all that was a blast—insights came, experiences were had, minor transformations happened.

Then I came upon the teachings of non-duality and thought I'd hit the jackpot. Tales of sudden awakenings and the end of suffering brought hope at a time of deep despair and anguish. The idea of no self particularly appealed to me. It seemed obvious that my self was the problem and that if I got rid of it, I'd be fine. I read books, watched videos, went to meetings, and longed for the moment of grace, the event that would finally deliver me from the prison of me.

One day, again while walking my dog, I saw clearly that I'm not the problem. More than that, I realized that there's never been a problem. Such relief; nothing to change, nowhere to go, no improvements to make. For a few days, I lived from that space. All the movements of life continued—thoughts came and went, emotions happened, bodily sensations arose. The *only* difference was that I was absolutely clear that none of it was a problem. Gradually, however, my belief in a deficient, suffering self returned and I struggled to find my way back to that spacious clarity.

Many of us initially relate to Scott Kiloby's notion of the core deficiency story because we believe ourselves to be deficient. I certainly did. When we're in that place, it's nearly impossible to see past our thoughts, feelings, and bodily sensations. We come up with all the evidence necessary that we are, indeed, what we believe ourselves to be: unloved, uncared for, victimized, not good enough, stupid. It wasn't until I began to look more closely at my basic assumption that, "Of course there's a problem or I wouldn't feel like this," that I began to see how flimsy the house of deficiency cards actually is.

Recently, I had a session with one of my fellow Living Inquiry facilitators to look for The Problem. Unsurprisingly, what emerged was a deep belief that I'm the problem. I sobbed. The wetness of the tears wasn't the problem. The energy of emotion in my body wasn't the problem. The words "it's me" weren't the problem. The sense of me wasn't the problem. After an hour, it became obvious; there is no problem anywhere to be found. From that perspective, it was crystal clear that even suffering, pain, and distress are not the problem that we presume them to be. There is nothing wrong with any of it; even the belief that there's a problem isn't a problem.

I've facilitated many inquiries now and been facilitated many times too. Whatever we've looked for, we've never found anything other than thoughts, images, emotions, and sensations. Even though the problem always seems real at the start of the session ("I need to lose weight," "She's better than me," "I'm unsupported," "I'm going to die"), its ultimately insubstantial nature is always apparent by the time we finish. Our assumptions are gently revealed by the process, and all the pain that we've been avoiding or trying to assuage is brought to light. We cry. We laugh. We experience insights and realizations. At the end of the process, we unerringly come back to the space in which everything arises, everything is known, nothing is judged, and nothing could ever be a problem.

On Making Resolutions (or Not)

Making New Year's resolutions has been going on for centuries; it is a time of new starts, of becoming better. There are some interesting resolution statistics: while only eight percent are successful in achieving their aim permanently, nearly half manage to do so for six months. People who make their goals specific ("I'll lose a pound a week" rather than "I'll lose weight") are ten times more likely to succeed. Those in their twenties are nearly three times more successful than those over fifty. The top ten resolutions are heartwarming; along with weight loss, smoking cessation, spending less, getting more organized, and getting fitter, we also vow to enjoy life to the fullest, help others in their dreams, fall in love, learn something exciting, and spend more time with family.

I was excited to discover the seventy resolutions of eighteenth-century New England preacher Jonathan Edwards. Written in the 1720s, his resolutions and subsequent commentary are so reminiscent of many of our own, albeit in the language of his day. He resolves to be the best possible Christian that he can, be nice to his parents, be even-tempered with everyone, live life to the full, eat and drink moderately, and be true to his faith in every detail. His earnestness and sincerity shine through every word; the ideal self that he constructs and then tries to live up to is palpable. He resolves to inquire every night—and at the end of every week, month, and year—whether he could have done better in any regard. And, like all of us, he often finds himself severely wanting:

> This week, have been unhappily low in the weekly account; and what are the reasons of it? Abundance of listlessness and sloth; and, if this should continue much longer, I perceive that other sins will begin to discover themselves. It

used to appear to me, that I had not much sin remaining; but now, I perceive there are great remainders of sin.[*]

As I sat, nearly three hundred years later, reading this young man's words, I was deeply moved by the knowledge that we're still grappling with that same cycle. We want to be better than we perceive ourselves to be, we create an ideal that we resolve to attain, and then we berate ourselves when we don't live up to or become our ideal. This is the territory of the superego, the part of the personality structure that creates and wants perfection and acts as the internal critic. The promptings of the superego can be useful when it acts as our conscience, and may stop us from acting out in harmful or damaging ways. The superego can also be harsh and vindictive, blaming and shaming us for not being who we're supposed to be. We've nearly all cowered before its criticisms: "You always were useless; look, you can't even manage a simple thing like that." Until we start to investigate further, we tend to believe the voice of the superego and its commentary, just as we believed our parents or early caregivers when we were young.

Inquiry gives us the means to deeply question the superego's assertions about us and who we are. Rather than trying to get out from under it, or trying to prove it wrong or right, take a while to simply listen to what it's saying. You'll begin to notice themes, of course. Your superego will tell you that you're X or Y, and that you need to do, or not do, A or B. As you listen to and look at its words, also begin to notice what's happening in your body. Sensations, feelings, emotions, or energies may well accompany the words that you're hearing or seeing. There will most likely be mental images or pictures; an image of you looking better in some way or some visual representation of the superego ideal. Notice, too, whether you feel compelled to comply; listen for "should" and "ought" and "must" and "must not."

---

[*]   Jonathan Edwards, "Saturday evening, Jan 5th 1723," *The Works of Jonathan Edwards Vol I and II*, Jonathan Edwards Collection, Beinecke Rare Book and Manuscript Library.

This is not about making this part of you wrong in some way. We don't have to get rid of or silence this inner voice. The superego develops naturally and is an essential part of the personality. As we inquire, it tends to change a little, lose its harshness, and take its rightful place. We're no longer at its mercy in the same way, feeling belittled or humiliated by it. The swings of the "I'm doing well" and "I'm doing badly" pendulum becomes gentler and we may then find a deeper level of resolve to do what feels right for ourselves.

Here's the thing: the superego believes that nothing can or will happen without its involvement. It believes that it is utterly necessary and that without it we will be inert or paralyzed or otherwise incapable of functioning. Like a negative and nagging coach, it believes that we'll never achieve anything without its constant exhortations.

What we discover is the opposite. When we inquire into its commands and demands, and meet the associated emotions and energies, and when we look at all its words and images, and gently dismantle its beliefs about us and who we are, we find that we're more, not less, able to change and achieve. Once the ideal self no longer holds any allure, we're more able to become who we are rather than who we think we should be.

So whether you resolve or not, there is always the opportunity to be with whatever's here. Right now, there are thoughts to look at (the words and mental images passing through your mind's eye) and feelings in the body (a tightness in my chest, the feeling of my cold fingers typing) to simply be noticed and felt. Make a resolution to rest in the present moment, even for a few seconds at a time, and see what evolves, resolves, dissolves, or solves from there.

On Resting (Again)

The urge to change, manage, fix, or control our experience runs deep. We're also prone to trying to control or fix the experience and behavior of those around us. We've been taught from an early age—and encouraged as adults—to make it better, to progress, to improve, to get somewhere. Whatever the perceived goal, be it wealth, happiness, health, enlightenment, power, the movement is the same. We have to get from *this* to *that*.

The notion of rest thus runs counter to many of our beliefs. When Scott Kiloby first started talking about rest, the idea left me flummoxed. For a while, I thought he was talking about relaxation. I'd spent many years unsuccessfully attempting to relax, and as many anxious people will attest, an instruction to relax often elicits the opposite response, only underlining the hypervigilance that seems impossible to turn off. I thought that the suggestion to rest meant that I should be relaxed and that therefore I wasn't getting it, I was doing something wrong. My underlying deficiency stories, "There's something wrong with me," and "I'm irretrievably damaged," were further confirmed.

As I looked at those and many other stories, I began to experience what Scott was actually referring to when he talked about rest. There's such a profound difference between having an intellectual or conceptual understanding of rest and experiencing it directly. Once I'd let go of trying to understand it, I started to feel it. And what struck me was the absolute simplicity of the instruction. *Let this be.* This simple noticing of what's already here: the thoughts, the mental images, the feelings and sensations in the body. *Be this, whatever this is.* After many years of trying to change, fix or manage *this*, there's a deep surrender in just being whatever we are in the moment. There's such effort and energy tied up in trying to not be what we are and to let that come to rest even for a few moments is transformational.

I also thought that rest was something I should do, an activity that I should be scheduling, like meditation. I'd always struggled with practice of any kind and I interpreted the suggestion to rest as an addition to my to-do list. After a while, I realized that I can rest in the midst of whatever is here—sitting on a train typing, talking with friends, lying on my bed and crying. Rest is always an option, whatever we're doing or feeling. It's simply taking a moment to be as we are, to notice and feel what's here in our experience. Right now, there's the movement of the train, my fingers on the keyboard, the sound of a crying child, the green of the countryside in my peripheral vision, a feeling of tightness in my abdomen, and thoughts of the family members that I've visited this weekend. I take a moment to pause, to let it all be exactly as it is. Nothing needs to be done with any of it, and yet, if something needs to be done—if I need to respond or react—that will happen, too.

The act of resting itself can also bring further underlying beliefs and fears to the surface. "If I'm not this, then what am I?" "Without this fear, I'll be undefended." "Without this compulsion, I'll be empty." "Without this anger, I'll be unable to act." We ascribe cause and purpose to our feelings and sensations, as if without them we won't be able to do or be. When we stop our strategizing and analyzing, even for a few seconds at a time, we get to experience what's actually here. And as we do that repeatedly, little by little, we begin to get more comfortable in this, even if it's really uncomfortable.

There's a paradox at work here, of course. As we give up our attempt to not be *this* and to become *that*, both seem to become interchangeable. As if we no longer mind which we are. As if there is no longer a distance between A and B, no route to travel. I'm not talking here about a nihilistic settling for or capitulation or resignation. I'm talking about a genuine okayness with whatever's here. And with that, there can be a real sense of movement, too. When we give up the striving to be or become what we're not, and simply are as we are, we often find ourselves becoming—with no effort involved. It has been a long time since I tried to relax; I've finally been allowing all those sensations and feelings that I called "stress" or "tension." And I'm the most relaxed I've ever been.

On Realizing the Political is Personal

We're all familiar with the play of oppositional, fear-fueled politics. Don't elect *them*. *They* will damage you or threaten your lifestyle or your life in some way. Whether it's other political parties, other countries, a particular group, or a kind of people, the dynamic is the same: there's *them* and there's *us* and never the twain shall meet. In the early 1970s, feminists coined the phrase, "The personal is political." I'd suggest that the reverse is also true: the political is personal.

Since I was young, I've sided with the underdog. I've worked and lived in disadvantaged inner-city areas. I've expressed disdain for the one percent, the bankers, the flagrantly rich. As I looked with another facilitator, an underlying story became very apparent. I saw the words, "I have to be modest." In addition to the words, there was a strong sensation and numerous images. Not only was there a self here who has to be modest, but also a command or instruction to be modest. I began to see how this played through in many areas of my life.

I don't yet know how seeing through this story of having to be modest will play out. We look, and see what follows from the looking. There's no prescription here. Whatever happens from now on, I'm no longer carrying that previously unconscious story of having to be modest, which was understandably triggered by images of people living in grand, distinctly immodest opulence. I no longer need to project it onto others; if it arises again, I'll most likely be aware of it. If not, I can simply inquire further.

Wherever you sit in the political landscape, take a look at those you think of as *them*, whoever they are. Whoever you hate, passionately disagree with, campaign against, or shout at when you're watching the news. Be it the political right, left or center, Muslims or Jews, black people or white people, refugees, feminists, pedo-philes, the religious right, the religious of any shade, those in same-sex relationships, immigrants, Darwinists, homophobes—this isn't about deciding who is right or wrong, but looking at how and where the political is personal.

Rest for a few moments, close your eyes, settle into your body, and take a couple of breaths. Then bring an image of *them* to mind and have a look at it. Simply look. Judgments about *them* may well arise. That's okay. We can come to those later. For now, see the image there in your mind's eye and see if it's a threat or danger or attack—find the word that fits the best. Remember, this isn't an intellectual or cognitive process; let your body give you the answer. If it responds in some way, it perceives a threat. However the response comes (as a sensation of tightness or contraction, a feeling of fear, some kind of emotion), let the response happen just as it's happening. Take time to feel it. And then let the process unfold, looking at the words and images that arise, and feeling the sensa-tions and feelings. See exactly where the threat lies, going by your body each time.

You may also notice that a self-identity arises in response to the perceived threat. You may notice words like "I'm under attack" or "They want to take something away from me" or "I'm inferior or superior to them." Look for that self, too.

It may also be useful to use the Boomerang or Panorama Inquiries here. We use the Boomerang to inquire into one triggering person or situation and the Panorama for looking at more than one.

When we project qualities onto others, be they positive or nega-tive, there's nearly always a deficient self-identity in play. Again, rest and bring an image of *them* to mind. As you look at *them*, see what the image of them says about you and who you are. Who are you in relation to them? Ask the question and listen for the answer. Ask several times, as different answers may come each time. See which one resonates in your body most and continue looking for that self in the words, images, and body sensations and feelings that arise.

Using the Inquiries in this way helps to defuse the fear and sense of threat around any political issue. Even things that seem inherently real—global warming, refugee crises, financial crises, whatever you feel affected by or preoccupied with—can be inquired into in this way. Leave no stone unturned. To inquire isn't to deny the existence of things or to arrive at a conclusion about them; it is simply to explore our experiences of them and to see where there are unexamined assumptions and beliefs operating.

When we're looking in this way, we can let go of any notion of being politically, emotionally, or spiritually correct. The Inquiries allow us to be gut-level honest in any given moment. We may be shocked or embarrassed by what comes—that's all part of the process. If there are places we dare not tread, we can look. What's the worst that could happen if we look at these words or images, or feel these feelings?

When we take the time to disentangle the personal from the political, we often find there's more clarity, flow, and spaciousness around our opinions. Perhaps we discover that the anger we've always felt toward the other side actually stems from an unconscious deficiency story. Or we find that we've aspired to be like our parents in order to gain their approval, sidelining our authentic selves in the process. Whatever we discover, we're left free to hold whatever views make sense to us, minus the rigidity that comes from fear or deficiency.

On Becoming Your Own Authority

One of the things I love about the Living Inquiries is that we start each session exactly where we are. Whether we're ranting, raving, and emotional, or feeling frustrated and all bottled up, or are calm and tranquil—that's where we begin. As the client, that's a gift in itself because I don't have to pretend or make an attempt to be anything other than I am in that moment. As the facilitator, it's also a gift because I can simply be present to the client just as they are, without any need or desire to change their experience in any way.

All of us have read, listened to, and heard many types of teaching or advice on how we should be and how we should live. When we get caught up in trying to figure out which practice or teaching we should follow, we can spiral into frantic self-doubt, panic, or helpless despair. Likewise, when we're trying to follow a teaching, believing that someone else has it all worked out, we can end up disillusioned and exhausted. It takes a lot of effort to try to not be what we are.

Wherever the teaching or advice is coming from—a guru or spiritual teacher, a self-help author or self-improvement expert, a health practitioner, or someone closer to home—when we take on the words of others as gospel, we usually end up suffering in some way or another. This may be because we feel we don't fully understand what they're saying or can't put it into practice or live up to it in some way. It may be because we compare ourselves to the other, nearly always unfavorably. We measure ourselves against the words of the other and find ourselves deficient. Clients often say to me, "I know I should..." or "I ought to X, but..." or "I've read that this spiritual teacher says we must..."

I've done it myself, of course. There was a time when I was beside myself, desperately trying to work out whose path I should follow to end the pain I was suffering. Once I began using the Living Inquiries, the motivation to follow someone else's teachings began to wane. The need to find advice or even salvation from outside of myself began to dissipate, and I began to trust the process itself like never before.

Once we begin to trust the process, we're able to rest with what's actually here, without the belief that anything should be any different. That's when insights tend to effortlessly arise and we discover the truth, in that moment, for ourselves.

When we perceive someone else as an authority, it's usually to our own detriment. Of course, it's wonderful that so many teachers share their insights and wisdom. However, insights, by their very nature, come from within. It doesn't matter how many times I share my insights with you or you with me, it's only when an insight arises spontaneously that we get to fully understand it from the inside out. While I love and treasure the insights that arise in sessions, I also know that there's no need to hang onto them. Once the moment of insight has happened and been fully experienced, that's it. Any attempt to turn that wonderful moment of understanding into a solid something—a creed or teaching—misses the point.

The insights I've had, whether I share them with you or not, don't make me a better (or worse) or more (or less) spiritual person. My writings may inspire you, irritate you, touch something within you, or illuminate something for you. What they don't do is to make me an authority. To pretend that was the case would be a disservice to us both. Whatever the insights I've had, they're meaningless in comparison to simply being present here with you, exactly as you are in this moment. But don't take my word for it. Have a look for yourself and become your own authority.

On Desire and Pleasure

A while ago, I found that I was using television as a way to switch off and withdraw from engagement with just being. It wasn't an all-out, rip-roaring compulsion, but I wanted a facilitated inquiry session to get to the bottom of what was going on. At one point in the session, a memory came up. I could see myself in the living room, aged twelve or thirteen, watching "Alias Smith and Jones." I loved those guys; I had my first celebrity crush on Ben Murphy, the actor who played Kid Curry. As I looked at the image, a feeling coursed through my body and it took me a while to name it. It was sheer, unadulterated pleasure of a kind I hadn't felt for a long time. It came as a revelation; I had no idea that I'd unconsciously associated watching television with such visceral pleasure.

We've nearly all been brought up in cultures which view at least some aspects of desire and pleasure as suspect. Certainly, the monotheistic religions have had much to say on the subject. Religious leaders the world over, for hundreds of years, have preached against the evils of too much pleasure and the dangers of giving in to our desires, be they for sex, music, dancing, food, drink, or other types of sensual pleasure. Many of us have studied aspects of Buddhism, which talks about attachment to desire being at the root of suffering. Spirituality has long been associated with asceticism, which gives up worldly, sensual pleasures in favor of an austere but transcendent existence. We've been taught, on many levels, that we can't have both, that there is a fundamental choice to be made between our lowly, animalistic, even uncontrollable desires or a higher, more worthy, existence that overcomes those desires and eschews physical pleasure.

The thing is, whatever we repress or disown doesn't conveniently disappear. It finds its way to the surface, often in unexpected and unwanted forms, including addiction and compulsion. Our inability to fully inhabit our bodies or fully accept our physical forms, because we've been led to believe that there's something fundamentally wrong or bad about our bodies and what they want, doesn't make us more spiritual. Denying our desires for what truly gives us pleasure doesn't make us better people. Far from it, we become fearful, sad, angry, and unfulfilled, and are left searching for something more to fill the hole that we feel inside.

The Living Inquiries give us a radical way to explore all of this fully. Take a look to see what it is that you really desire. Does it mean something about you that you desire it? As the words and images come, feel into your body's response to them. Follow the trail and see where it leads. You can also look for the self that desires, the self that wants pleasure. Do these desires pose a threat? There are so many paths to explore and such richness in the looking. Inquiring with a facilitator can help if you're unfamiliar with the process.

As my journey with the Living Inquiries continues, I find myself naturally doing more and more of the things that give me pleasure. The taboos around pleasure and desire have loosened. I can still feel a little puritanical judgment within me at times and, when I do, I often inquire. When I allow myself pleasure, I know that I feel more alive. The sinuousness of the right bassline. The movement in my limbs as I dance. The sumptuousness of the water as I dive down below the surface. That indescribable taste of chocolate. A good movie on a quiet evening after work. Any notion that there is a division between the spiritual and the material has all but dissolved. It's becoming more and more pleasurable to simply be here.

On Investigating the Equations We Live By

I didn't take my first airplane flight until I was twenty-seven and already prone to anxiety and over-anticipation. Not surprisingly, I found it terrifying and spent most of the ensuing week trying not to think about the return journey. From that point on, I was convinced that flying is frightening and that my only possible response to it could be fear.

We take on fixed views on a whole range of subjects. Ourselves and who we are: "I've always been like that," "That's just how I am." Other people, both people we know and those we don't: "Conservatives are mean and hard-hearted," "My aunt's always been a saint." We carry lists around with us about the things that make us anxious, the things that we have to have or can't survive without. We think we know how things are, as if life is totally immutable and unchangeable.

In one of my favorite passages in Scott Kiloby's book *The Living Inquiry,* he describes what he calls the "scandal of objectivity." We believe that things are as we see them and so we are incapable of seeing them in any other way. This is not, of course, a new idea. The saying "We don't see things as they are, we see them as we are," has been a popular quote for centuries. The implications of this in each of our lives are far-reaching. If we see ourselves as unwanted or unloved, for example, we will view every interaction with others through this lens. If we believe that we must have tobacco, that we're incapable of functioning without it, we will organize our lives accordingly. If we believe that anxiety is the only possible response to a given situation, we'll doubtless be anxious. If we see others as mean or unkind, we'll react as if that's the case regardless of how they're behaving toward us.

When we explore these entrenched beliefs using the Living Inquiries, we begin to see that they are shaped purely from within. Whatever has happened to us in the course of our lives, the beliefs we hold are made up of the thoughts (words and images) and feelings (sensations, emotions and other bodily energies) that we experience. It's the combination of thoughts and feelings together that makes our beliefs so convincing—yet when we look at or feel each element on its own, we begin to notice its ephemeral, fleeting nature.

When we're compulsive or addicted, for example, we believe that we have to do or have something in order to function or survive. The compulsion or addiction feels like an absolute necessity; we can't take it or leave it. Using the Inquiries, we look much more closely and directly at the mechanism driving our behavior. What, exactly, is telling us that we have to do or have this thing? What is actually compelling us? By taking each component one by one, we get to examine in forensic detail the *where* and *how* of the addiction or compulsion itself. For example, we may find that an energy in the stomach or chest seems to drive the compulsive movement, or that there's a belief about ourselves that we're desperate to block out. We may discover a deep-rooted fear that's being kept at bay by the addictive behavior. Whatever our findings, the assumptions that have underpinned our actions become less solid and real. Once the foundations start to crumble, it's inevitable that the compulsive or addictive behaviors begin to change.

It can be frightening to discover that we're not who we thought we were or that our most cherished beliefs and assumptions don't stand up to scrutiny. It can feel, momentarily, as if the devil we know is preferable to the one we don't. That's part of the process of inquiring and is totally natural. We simply investigate further to see what it is we're assuming lies in wait for us. Ultimately, we'll find more words, images, and sensations.

When we are willing to look deeply and consistently, we begin to see the world without the shroud of our beliefs and assumptions, which is a true gift. Everything—including ourselves and others—is then free to be itself without the burden of the meaning that we've

On Learning How
to Make and
Break Our Habits

In habit formation, automaticity is the point at which a habit becomes automatic; we find ourselves doing it unconsciously or, at least, without much thought. Automaticity is a hallmark of compulsion or addiction; we come to our senses, as it were, when the ice cream is already half-eaten or when we've smoked most of the pack. The habitual nature of compulsions makes them seem harder to break.

A few years ago, researchers at University College London found that, on average, it took sixty-six days for a habit to become entrenched to the point of automaticity. The research participants were building up positive habits, such as drinking more water or eating a piece of fruit after lunch. For some, it took only eighteen days. For others, it was much, much longer: 254 days or thirty-six weeks. The researchers also found that the occasional missed day didn't make any difference, which is a relief since we often imagine that if we skip even one day, we'll end up back at square one. But this clearly isn't the case.[*]

There's apparently physiological truth to the saying, "Old habits die hard." In 2005, researchers at MIT reported that "Important neural activity patterns in a specific region of the brain change when habits are formed, change again when habits are broken, but quickly reemerge when something rekindles an extinguished

---

[*] UCL News, "How long does it take to form a habit?," August 4, 2009, accessed May 3, 2016, https://www.ucl.ac.uk/news/news-articles/0908/09080401.

habit—routines that originally took great effort to learn."** We've all experienced this in some way, either with an activity like riding a bicycle, or more detrimentally, with habits like smoking or drinking.

The thing that really caught my eye as I was reading about the London research was the scale used to measure automaticity. The Self-Report Habit Index*** covers twelve items, as follows:

Behavior X is something...

1. I do frequently.

2. I do automatically.

3. I do without having to consciously remember.

4. that makes me feel weird if I do not do it.

5. I do without thinking.

6. that would require effort not to do it.

7. that belongs to my (daily, weekly, monthly) routine.

8. I start doing before I realize I'm doing it.

9. I would find hard not to do.

10. I have no need to think about doing.

11. that's typically "me."

12. I have been doing for a long time.

** MIT News, "Brain researchers explain why old habits die hard," October 19, 2005, accessed May 3, 2016, http://news.mit.edu/2005/habit.

*** Verplanken, B. and Orbell, S., "Reflections on Past Behavior: A Self-Report Index of Habit Strength," *Journal of Applied Social Psychology* 33(6), (2003), quoted in "Habits," Consumer Health Informatics Research Resource (CHIRr), accessed May 3, 2016, http://chirr.nlm.nih.gov/habits.php.

As I pondered this list, I realized that the practices of Natural Rest and the Living Inquiries, particularly the Compulsion Inquiry, address various points in this index. Take number 3, for example. We know from our work that what we call the "ghost image" is invariably involved in the movement toward the substance or behavior, but it often goes unnoticed—which is precisely why we call it the "ghost" image. A little like subliminal advertising, it is a fleeting image or mental picture that seems to prompt or remind us to reach out for the substance or behavior. It could be an image of a cold beer or the ice cream in the freezer; if we can spot the ghost image and look directly at it, we can become more conscious of our actions, thus reducing the habit's automaticity. This inquiry question also helps: Is this image commanding me or compelling me to do X?

Numbers 4 and 9 are also addressed directly by this work. "Feeling weird" happens because we've used the habit to medicate or move away from uncomfortable feelings or emotions. By becoming aware of, staying with, and further exploring the "weird" feelings, we have less need to engage in the habit. We discover that there are other ways to be with uncomfortable feelings and energies, and we break the link between the two. Equally, we explore why it's "hard not to do X." Usually, it's because if we didn't do it, we'd have to feel or experience something that we don't want to feel or that we believe would be unbearable in some way. As we begin to open to whatever we've been closed to, to welcome these feelings and let them be, it feels easier to not do X.

Number 11 is also an area that we address head-on in Living Inquiries sessions. We discover the exact nature of this "me" in relation to the habit. It's usually a story of self-deficiency, for example, of being unloved, not enough, or incapable. We then look to see if we can find this "me." During this process, we discover, look at, and feel all those parts of the seeming "me" that have been hooked into the habit, which further weakens the link between the two. As we become more aware of our beliefs, thoughts, sensations and feelings, we slowly move out of automaticity.

On Objectifying Our Selves, Others, and the World

During one facilitated inquiry, I suddenly saw that there was space where I'd always assumed my mind to be. My immediate response was laughter. Afterward, I was struck by the fact that I had believed in the solid existence of this "mind" object, as if it was separate from me. *Me and my mind.*

This basic split of me versus not-me lies at the heart of our sense of who we are. I'm *me*—the subject in here, and everything else is an object in my purview. I objectify everything that surrounds me and proceed to relate to it all as if I am entirely separate. Our subject/object relationships can be the source of both pleasure and suffering. There are objects that: I want but haven't got; I have and want to keep; I have but don't want; are doing something pleasurable, disturbing, or painful to me.

We objectify everything: inanimate and animate physical objects, including other individuals or groups of people, as well as concepts and abstractions. We create objects, posit them outside ourselves, and proceed to relate to them from our subjective perspective. We also objectify our selves, our bodies, and parts of ourselves. We objectify ourselves as a particular thing: "I'm a loser" or "I'm a victim" or "I'm a lesbian." We divide ourselves even further, experiencing the subject/object dynamic internally as well as externally: "I hate myself," "I'm ashamed of myself," "I'm proud of myself." Operating within this terrain leaves us, as the subject, with no option but to attempt to manage and control all the objects that surround us as best we can.

Our assumption that we know what someone or something is allows us to act accordingly. If I believe that you are worthless and undeserving, I will treat you as such, and vice versa. We see the dire consequences of objectification all around us in misunderstandings, online and offline bullying, sexual violence and abuse, racism, sexism, homophobia, transphobia, and disablism—all these forms stem from that same root. In the extreme, war, ethnic cleansing, and holocausts result; whole tribes or nations utterly dehumanized and objectified by those who see them as scapegoats, vermin, or worse.

While the majority of us do not act toward others with such a lack of humanity, it is humbling and instructive to inquire into our own patterns of objectification. Given that none of us are immune to cultural mores and pressures, we internalize numerous messages about how we, as objects, are supposed to be and then judge ourselves according to how we measure up. Likewise, we judge those around us, attempting to change them to conform more closely to how we believe they should be.

Inquiring gives us the opportunity to look more closely at both subject and object. We can simply look for the object itself and we can look for anything that we can name, so the possibilities are almost infinite: mother, father, son, daughter, wife, husband, lover, boss, guru, friend, Republicans, liberals, the rich, refugees, fundamentalist Christians, terrorists, my body, my mind, my ego, and so on. As we begin to look, we discover that our chosen object is made up of the elements of our experience of it, both in the mind through words and images, and in the body through sensations, emotions, and other types of feeling or sensory experiencing. As we look at or feel each element, we ask the simple question: Is this X? A bodily response—be it emotion, feeling, or some unnamable contraction or sensation—gives us a yes, indicating that there is more to unfold.

As the looking continues, we begin to see how our experience of the object in question is inseparable from the object itself, that our experience of it is not the object itself, and that the object cannot possibly be separate from our experience of it. Then the subject/object divide begins to dissolve. We're then less prone to what Scott Kiloby calls "outward pointing," which is finding fault or making judgments or criticisms about others, as if we're objectively correct.

This isn't to say that we no longer have opinions nor that we begin to tolerate bad behavior or abuse from others. We're simply freed from the illusions that objects exist out there, entirely independently from us and that they intrinsically are as we see them. The objects are freed from having to be what we see them as and can instead be what they are. This shift in perspective can create profound changes in our relationships.

Inquiring into abstract ideas is also liberating. Concepts such as love, trust, peace, truth, evil, God, enlightenment, and awakening can all be investigated. We tend to reify such concepts in a phenomenon known as "the fallacy of misplaced concreteness," believing them to be solid and attainable objects that we are either in possession of or not. We use capitals to denote their solidity, referring to Truth or Peace or Love. We then measure our progress, or lack thereof, accordingly. I once worked with a client to look for the self who couldn't reach his full potential. Once we looked for "potential" and the whole concept fell apart, the self who couldn't reach it became moot.

These investigations unfold in a way that's utterly unique in each session. We can't possibly foretell what we'll discover or what associations will emerge. We often find ourselves beyond the parameters of our existing knowledge, way beyond our beliefs. What we do know is that, after looking, we're able to relate to the object in question—be it an abstract notion, a dearest loved one, or a *bête noire*—with more lightness, in the knowledge that the object is far more and far less than we've believed it to be.

On Letting Things Take Their Place

For decades, I seemed to be defined by my emotions, sensations, fears, and compulsions. Every day saw me navigating through each of these, evaluating relative successes and failures. A lack or absence of fear was always deemed a good thing. I'd keep count of the number of cigarettes I'd smoked or the amount of food I'd eaten—subdividing, of course, into the healthy and not-healthy categories—and judge myself accordingly. Success seemed to lie in my ability to control my feelings. I'd swing between triumphant and despondent depending on whether I'd managed to do so or not, and my self-esteem would vary accordingly.

A boyfriend once remarked that I seemed to be a victim of my emotions, a comment that I took badly at the time. However, if we're honest, I think many of us have felt that we're at the mercy of seemingly uncontrollable waves of feelings, sensations, and energies. Fear, anger, sadness, shame, anxiety—whatever the exact nature of the feeling—we'll do our utmost to stem its tide by whatever means necessary. And those means cover a wide range of behaviors like drinking alcohol, overeating, under-eating, medicating with prescription or social drugs, shopping, spiritual seeking. The list goes on as we find a multitude of ways to avoid being with what's here. In essence the feelings or sensations that we're running from are running the show, whether we like to admit it or not.

As we start to look more closely, several things become apparent. One is that we inevitably do not want to feel what we're feeling. Another is that it often seems as if the feelings will become overwhelming if we don't control or avoid them. And it can feel as if the feelings will go on forever if we simply let them be there—which seems intolerable. We also become aware of how deeply exhausting it is to resist and attempt to control our experience in this way, and we long to stop, even as we fear the consequences of doing so.

The Living Inquiries and Natural Rest give us a way to explore all of this much more deeply. By allowing each layer of experience to be exactly as it is, we're able to penetrate the sometimes dense and intense energies or feelings that we've been avoiding. We stay with the feelings of not wanting and resistance, letting them be. We look at the threat of finally feeling all that's here. "What's the worst that can happen if I feel this?" Various answers may come and each one is looked at, listened to, felt into, and given full permission to be as it is. We start to touch on the exhaustion itself and take moments here and there to rest more fully.

As this happens, we find ourselves less defined and driven by the feelings, sensations, and energies that we've been trying to control or avoid. The tightness in the chest, emptiness in the belly, sadness, anger—whatever it is—can be felt here and now, just as it is. The reaching out and the moving away begin to settle, the compulsive behaviors start to quiet. Our lives and the decisions we make are not predicated on avoidance or resistance anymore. We're able to tolerate and even welcome our present experience. The feelings, sensations, emotions, and energies that we've been managing, resisting, or avoiding can then take their natural place, freed from the burden of controlling our lives. Here are the words that came to me when I realized this:

> I come to a stop
> At first, it's hard to breathe
> As wants, needs, fears, ifs, and buts
> (The things I thought were me)
> Implore me to go on
> Much like a clamoring, mewling litter
> From this silent dwelling place
> I hear their sweet cries
> And gently greet them, one by one
> Shrill though they can be
> They never actually wanted to run the show

On Noticing Our Needs

I've thought a lot about need, and how need, want, desire, and compulsion often become bound up together in a confusing way. We often say that we "need" something as if it were essential to our survival, when clearly it's not. And we often have no idea of what it is we really need.

As young children, our needs sometimes went unmet. Even the best parents are sometimes unattuned to their children and many of us have experienced shades of neglect or worse. We often find it hard to name or identify what we need, let alone ask for it. So we reach out for substances or become fixated on activities that we feel or believe will give us what we need.

I once worked with a client using the Compulsion Inquiry to look at overeating. We reached a point in the session when she connected deeply with her childhood longing for love. She saw an image of herself as a little girl, reaching out her arms. As she looked at this and other memories, and felt the long-buried feelings, she was able to connect with a love far more powerful than she'd felt before, coming from within. Her compulsion reduced after she realized that food didn't contain the love that she needed.

After smoking for many years, off and on, eventually I became more and more curious about my seemingly addictive behavior. I concluded early on that I wasn't physiologically addicted, as I could easily go a number of days without smoking if the conditions were right. For example, if I was at home with my son, focused on being a mother and on my studies, I didn't feel like smoking. As soon as I was in a social setting or having an intimate or intense conversation with someone, I'd reach for the tobacco. I realized that for me, the smoking habit was related to my unmet and unacknowledged need for closeness or intimacy—and my simultaneous fear of it. Every time someone came close, I'd surround myself in a cloud of smoke. Interestingly, I finally stopped altogether shortly after beginning a long-distance relationship, which for a while fulfilled my need for connection without challenging my needs for space and autonomy. Once my need for connection had been met in a way that felt right, my need for tobacco fell away effortlessly.

One of the things I love about the Living Inquiries is the way that we discover, often very quickly, what lies behind our addictive or compulsive behaviors. By looking very specifically, as we do in the Living Inquiries, to see if we can find what is compelling us to use or act, we get to discover the needs that have been previously suppressed or unseen. There's no formula here, each session is a unique journey in itself, and yet there are common threads for all of us.

At their root, our compulsions are a misunderstanding, a mistake. We've come to believe that we're missing something, that we don't have something we need, and so we go looking for it in substances or activities. When we look, we discover that fundamentally there's nothing missing and that our needs, our totally understandable human needs, can or are being met without recourse to our substance or activity. We can also, if we're inclined, question the very notion of the self with needs. Where is the one who needs?

Paradoxically, when we dive right into the heart of our supposed needs and our neediness, we become much more able to do what's right and healthy for ourselves without being rigid about it. Simultaneously, we free ourselves from addictive or compulsive behavior.

On Letting It Be

As a Living Inquiries facilitator, I say the words "Let it be" many times a day. Whatever it is—searing grief, raging anger, uncontrollable laughter, tightness, stuck energy, resistance, moving energy, sadness—my only response is to be with my client in whatever they're experiencing, and let it be. We sit together, and we *let it be*. And every day, I'm moved by what happens in sessions. I'm moved beyond words by each client's courage, their willingness to feel it all, their willingness to face all those words and images that they've been resisting for so long. And I know that I can truly let it all be because I've been there, in my turn, over and over and over again.

During one self-facilitation, early in the session the words, "I had to keep myself company," came up and were accompanied by strong emotion. Then, images of the Living Inquiries community came to mind and I sobbed. Along with the emotion came the idea that the kindness I'd always longed for is here, amongst us. Strangers and friends, holding each other, letting it all be. Time and again, we open up to each other, the world over, to look at what we most dread, to share our most shameful secrets, to rest together with whatever's here, and to see that it's not what we thought it was— that we're not the damaged, unloved, incomplete, or lacking people that we've taken ourselves to be.

As Paul McCartney sang in "Let It Be," many of us are brokenhearted. And here, in this community, we have total permission to be as brokenhearted as we are. How can we not be, really? We've all loved and lost, we've all been rejected or abandoned, we've all been afraid, and we've all been scarred in some shape or form. We've all done our damnedest to cover up or escape from our brokenheartedness, too.

At last, we can rest right in it and let it be. And right there, in truly being brokenhearted, we get to see that it is all completely, utterly okay. That it was always okay, even when it felt intolerable or unbearable. Let's embrace our own and each other's brokenheartedness. Nothing to cure, nothing to remedy. The prescription here is simple yet wise: let it be. And with that can come the sweetest surrender and the discovery that it's all love, whatever its guise.

On Seeing through Suffering

We should make all spiritual talk
Simple today:
God is trying to sell you something,
But you don't want to buy.
That is what your suffering is:
Your fantastic haggling,
Your manic screaming over the price!

—Hafiz*

I used to suffer. A lot. It felt as if my suffering was deeper, more pro-found, and longer lasting than anyone else's. (I'm referring to non-physical suffering; I was acutely aware of the incomparable suffering of those with severe chronic pain or life-threatening medical condi-tions.) I remember sitting in a group-sharing session, listening to one of the participants talk about an issue that she was having with a colleague. Feeling a mix of contempt and envy, I was stunned that this was the most difficult thing in her life. I thought, *Try being plagued with anguish and panic, feeling like you're going to die any minute.* I spent a long time and a lot of energy trying to find ways to salve my suffering, trying to find the permanent solution that would finally bring it to an end. Needless to say, I was unsuccessful in this quest.

I assumed that, in order to be relieved of the suffering, I would have to eradicate all the troublesome feelings and thoughts. It didn't

* Hafiz poem "Manic Screaming" is from the Penguin publication *I Heard God Laughing: Poems of Hope and Joy.* Copyright © 1996 and 2006 by Daniel Ladin-sky and used with his permission.

occur to me that the suffering may be the result of the way that I was looking at what was happening, rather than the happenings themselves. When I came across spiritual teachings, my suffering appeared to intensify. The idea that I should be accepting or embracing what was going on added yet another layer of wrongness into the mix, as did the idea that it may be my thoughts that were creating the suffering itself.

My identity as a sufferer, "I am the one who suffers," wasn't in doubt until I started to investigate it more closely, using the Living Inquiries. Of course I was suffering, that was a given, and I had all the evidence from thoughts, memories, and intense emotions to back up that assumption. However, when I began to look at each of those components separately, as we do when we inquire, it became apparent that the sufferer wasn't as solid or real as I'd assumed her to be.

I looked at words: "I'm suffering," "This really hurts," "I'm the one who is unwanted." An endless stream of thoughts, all asserting their supposed truth. I started to see that the thoughts alone didn't constitute suffering.

Then came the images: memories, pictures of the future, my imaginings—some of them deeply painful. What I noticed was that the suffering came from the combination of words, images, and feelings (what Scott Kiloby calls the Velcro Effect), not simply from one single component. When I was able to look at each image on its own, to really look at it, I could see that the image, in itself, didn't mean anything about me. I also began to see that the presence of images or memories didn't actually constitute suffering.

My biggest revelation came when I was able to feel emotions and sensations without the words and images attached to them. I'd always taken it for granted that those feelings were the suffering. Stripped of their associations—the layers of meaning, it turned out that even intense emotions were bearable. More than that, they sometimes became pleasurable or at least neutral. Energy moving through the body and being felt. Indistinguishable from aliveness and no longer perceived as negative in any way. I discovered the breathtaking, exquisite beauty in sadness, the innocence of fear, the high of anger, stripped of connotations.

Going through the inquiry process, over and over again, the underlying belief that there was something wrong with what I was feeling, that sense of "I shouldn't be feeling like this," began to ebb away. Suffering, as Hafiz pointed out, comes not from life itself, but from our quibbling about it. By taking a look at each element of our experience, gently, curiously, and with courage, meeting all of it as it is, we untangle the tale of suffering, and the one who suffers is nowhere to be found.

I used to believe that my suffering would end when my feelings and thoughts were somehow magically transmuted into their opposites. It is delightful to discover that the end of suffering lies in those very same feelings and thoughts, exactly as they are. My life continues as it did, my feelings and thoughts come and go as they do, yet what was once considered suffering is now vital, alive, precious, and very much less serious than it used to seem.

On Taking a Look for Ourselves

I was fortunate enough to be brought up in a mercifully dogma-free church in which tolerance, equality, moderation, and debate were valued. The mild-mannered minister—part administrator, part guide and counsel—was a far cry from the God-appointed intermediary of some denominations, standing in judgment over the congregation. I stopped attending in my late teens, not because I disagreed with the content of the sermons, but because churchgoing was terminally uncool. It would be many years before I set foot in a church again, other than to attend a wedding or funeral or to admire the architecture.

Likewise, I was never very sold on the idea of the spiritual teacher. I'd see a picture of someone's guru and think *I'm not going to just take the word of some guy.* (The picture was usually of a man, with some notable exceptions). And yet, I was still searching. I toyed with a variety of teachings and practices, playing about on the periphery of most of them, never feeling drawn to devotion or even halfhearted commitment. I'd hear about experiences with Indian mystics and Western *advaita*, or nonduality, teachers, and feel a response that was part envy, part longing, part defensiveness. *Oh yeah? Really?* Despite my skepticism, I couldn't shake off the idea that there was an imperceptible difference between me and them, that they had something I didn't, that they had seen the invisible *That* to which I was still blinded.

I've read or heard many things from spiritual teachers that have touched me deeply. I've cried and laughed in spontaneous recognition of what Tony Parsons, Jeff Foster, John Wheeler, Gangaji, Rodney Stevens, Tim Freke, or Scott Kiloby have pointed out. And that's wonderful. For a while, though, I ascribed a great deal of weight to their words; I assumed that they had what I hadn't, that they were where I wasn't—yet. I hung on to phrases like "presence awareness," "the natural state," "no self," and "rest as awareness," contorting myself in attempts to see or reach or realize. It has to be said, this was largely to absolutely no avail. I felt frustrated, despairing, even a little aggrieved.

Meanwhile, I've cried and laughed and been deeply touched many times over by the wise words of any number of my friends. People whose names you won't recognize, whose words you wouldn't necessarily pay attention to, because you wouldn't consider them enlightened or awakened. In those moments, there's been no despair, frustration, or grief, because there's been no belief that they are anything more, or less, than I am.

Here's the thing: whenever we look to other people for our answer, we're looking in the wrong place. Yes, there are some lovely words out there, but they don't contain the golden ticket. There is no word, phrase, sentence, paragraph, or chapter that will remit your suffering and give you peace. Yes, there are people who appear to have ascended the heavenly staircase, who appear to have been given the keys to the kingdom. Good for them. If you listen to what many of them are saying, however, they're telling you to look deeply into your own experience. They say that they have nothing to give you, that there is nothing missing or incomplete about you.

I know how improbable, impossible, or unbelievable all that can sound. But here's the thing, again: we can only look within our own experience.

Happily for us all, we have a tried and tested method for this looking. During the past few years, we've looked at life from innumerable angles using the Living Inquiries. Generally speaking, all we find is a set of assumptions that consist of some beliefs, a concoction of words and images in the mind, which are stirred into a morass of feelings and sensations in the body that make it all feel real.

Even better news is that we don't need to have reached any particular state to look in this way and that there is nothing we need to understand intellectually about the process. It really is just looking. In fact, it's *so* simple that children can do it.

Here's the final thing: it is very helpful to look with someone else. There's something in the *sharing* of it all that is touching and intimate. There's a community forming around this, in which we're all looking, where there are no degrees of attainment despite the titles that we use. A community in which we're all equal, in which we're able to open up to each other to a degree that many of us have not experienced before. A community in which our lived experience is what counts and through which we're learning to trust the evidence of our senses rather than another's teaching. There is no advice here, no words of wisdom. There's simply an offer to look and see what is already here. The wonder is that we're all capable of this looking, regardless of what we believe. And that's the real golden ticket.

On the Innocence of the Inappropriate Pairing

When Scott Kiloby and Colette Kelso first developed the Compulsion Inquiry, one of their observations particularly impressed me. They noticed that a key component of the mechanism of compulsion is the projection of a desired or missing quality onto the substance or activity concerned. In other words, we feel as if we're missing or lacking something in ourselves and we believe that it is somehow contained within the substance or activity. In order to get it, we have to take the substance or do the activity. Scott and Colette call this mechanism "inappropriate pairing"—inappropriate because when we investigate further, we find that the pairing is based on a misconception or misunderstanding.

As I started to work with clients on compulsion and addiction, I saw the accuracy of this observation time and time again. At some point in the session, the client would realize that they assumed they could get love from food, or excitement, glamour, and vitality from smoking, or validation and power from pornography. It's not as if any of us are fully conscious of the inappropriate pairing before we really look; the lasting allure of the compulsion or addiction lies, after all, in the forlorn hope that maybe this time we'll finally get what we feel we need and the gnawing sense of lack will be laid to rest at last. It is an innocent mistake, born from the unexamined assumptions that we carry with us.

When I cut my foot on some broken glass and required stitches, I had the chance to experience inappropriate pairing firsthand. Almost immediately, and over the ensuing days, I watched my craving for dark chocolate and salted caramel ice cream arise again.

I got to see how my compulsions are intrinsically linked to trauma, a connection I hadn't seen with such clarity before. And then while I was being facilitated, I saw how I'd inappropriately and unconsciously paired chocolate and ice cream with stability, reliability, and certainty. An image of the supermarket shelves came up and as I looked, I began to see how I projected those qualities onto those items; always available, always there, always predictable. And in that moment, the struggles with food that started in my late teens made complete sense. Stability, reliability, and certainty were the very qualities that my life and I seemed to be totally lacking. No wonder I looked for them elsewhere, convinced that they weren't here.

Even more precious, I then realized the fundamental goodness or rightness of that compulsive movement. It wasn't actually wrong, as I'd assumed over the years. Having spent my late teens and early twenties viciously berating myself for my compulsive eating habits and trying to drill myself out of them, I finally got to see that the movement toward stability, reliability, and certainty was an attempt to give myself what I thought I needed—not a fundamental flaw or weakness. It was a simple case of misunderstanding and of misperception.

Once the inappropriate pairing is seen, its inappropriateness becomes obvious, as does the innocence of the assumption. For me, bringing to light the belief, along with its accompanying feelings—which were previously unconscious, was enough to create a significant shift. I haven't bought any more dark chocolate since. Walking past the chocolate aisle in the supermarket the other day brought no more than a slight sense of bewilderment at what all the fuss had been about. The half-eaten ice cream has remained in the freezer. Maybe one day I'll feel like having some.

On the Question of Choice

Choice is a thorny issue in recovery circles and spiritual communities. Notions of choice and free will are also the subjects of numerous neuroscience experiments. In the early 1980s, Benjamin Libet's experiments appeared to demonstrate that not all choice is made consciously. It seems that the conscious mind becomes aware of choices that have already been initiated elsewhere in the brain and body. From this perspective, our thinking minds may not be so much the makers of choice as the recipients of choices already made.

In general, we tend to think of our self—the "I" that we take ourselves to be—as the maker of choice, the decider. We cogitate long and hard over upcoming decisions or we berate ourselves for poor choices made in the past. We may believe that choices are made purely within thought or that they are also informed by emotional and bodily senses. We often have polarized views on choice, believing that we have no choice at all, or that there is no chooser, or that we're powerless to choose in certain areas of our lives. We may believe that our reality has been created solely by our personal choices and that we can manifest our heart's and mind's desires simply by making the right choices. Choices are viewed as right or wrong, good or bad, and are often agonized over.

I've experienced times in my life when it seemed I had no choice at all, as many of us do. As children, we often have no choice about what's happening in our families or our lives and that experience of choicelessness can reappear at various times throughout our lives. It can be deeply humbling to realize that we're not the authors of our lives, particularly if we've been controlling or convinced of our individual ability to direct the course of life according to our own will.

At such times, it appears that there is absolutely no choice but to do or undergo as life dictates. We may feel powerless, helpless, or relieved. There may be all sorts of accompanying emotions and stories about ourselves; shame, weakness, disgust, resistance. We may fight or surrender or both.

I've also experienced times when I've seemed to make very conscious choices, from small, mundane choices like what to wear to big, life-changing choices like leaving a relationship. At these times, the choice-making appears absolutely real, as if there's a choosing self here who has considered all the pros and cons of a particular decision and chosen accordingly. We may feel self-congratulatory or self-critical about our choice—either way, it feels unquestionable that we're the ones who have made it. It can also seem that no choice would get made without the choice-making activity; the weighing up, the mulling over, the cogitation.

Whatever our ideas or beliefs about choice are, it's an extremely fertile ground for inquiry. If you believe that you don't have a choice, investigate further. If you believe you do have a choice, take a look. Look for choice itself—along with the command to choose or not choose, or the threat in making a choice or not, or the wrongness or rightness of particular choices.

As we inquire, we look at words, see images, and feel bodily sensations and feelings, but ultimately we won't be able to find a separate self who can either choose or not choose. The inquiry process itself often yields rich insights and understandings along the way, as it's not about mentally arriving at the conclusion that there's no self. Rather a deep, experiential dive takes us into the heart of who we take ourselves to be. We come to see for ourselves how, even in the absence of a separate self, mysteriously and amazingly, choosing and not choosing happens and choices get made.

This isn't about arriving at a fixed conclusion or viewpoint. It isn't as if we walk away from a session with the belief that there's no one here to choose or not. The seeing of no self in the moment doesn't let us off the hook in any way. In fact, we become more, not less, able to take responsibility for our choices, both past and present. We see the ultimate innocence in all our choice-making, and yet are able to make better, healthier choices for ourselves.

I invite you to look for yourself.

On What Can We Really Depend?

A word that crops up frequently in relation to addiction is *dependency*. We consider ourselves to be dependent on the substance or activity of addiction. Those who are in relationships with addicts often refer to themselves as codependent. It struck me recently that maybe dependency, in its widest sense, plays an important role in addiction and compulsion.

It's well known that many people with problems of addiction or compulsion come from dysfunctional family backgrounds. As babies and children, we're profoundly dependent on those around us; if they had not provided us with life's basic necessities, we would have died. Even if our physiological needs are met and we're fed, sheltered, and kept warm, a lack of basic safety or love in those early years has a profound effect upon our development. As Abraham Maslow described in his theory of the hierarchy of needs,* our requirements for esteem, friendship, love, and security are fundamental. Interestingly, he called them the "deficiency needs," indicating that our deficiency stories, as Scott Kiloby calls them, emerge

---

* 1. Biological and physiological needs include air, food, drink, shelter, warmth, sex, sleep.
2. Safety needs include protection from elements, security, order, law, stability, freedom from fear.
3. Love and belongingness needs include friendship, intimacy, affection, love from work group, family, friends, romantic relationships.
4. Esteem needs include achievement, mastery, independence, status, dominance, prestige, self-respect, respect from others.
5. Self-actualization needs include realizing personal potential, self-fulfillment, seeking personal growth, peak experiences.

A.H. Maslow, "A theory of human motivation," *Psychological Review* 50(4), (1943): 370–96.

because these fundamental needs are not met. If there's nothing solid for us to depend on, if our environment is unsafe, abusive, or unloving, then it makes sense that we reach out for something that we can depend upon.

Many of us experience our first glimpse of addiction as teenagers and young adults. At that time, much as we may still be feeling our dependency needs, we're also loudly proclaiming our independence. "I don't need you," is the teenager's cry, and they're often loathe to admit any kind of dependency on others, especially their parents. More physically independent at this age, we're able to venture further out into the wider world, where we discover objects and activities on which to transfer our dependency needs. And there's a certain logic to this because cigarettes, alcohol, video games, porn and drugs are, in a way, dependable. They don't let us down, they don't abuse us, they don't behave like the people around us do. They give us what we expect of them, every time, even if it's not what we actually need.

Western culture highly values independence. It's easy to ignore our real need for dependence, to ignore our need for the basics of love, security, esteem, and friendship. As a young teenager, my parents separated after many years of unhappiness for all concerned. For at least a decade afterward, I frequently declared that, rather than damaging me in some way, this event had merely served to make me independent and had therefore done me a favor. I went about my life, not realizing that my compulsions of smoking and binge eating, in particular, were masking my real needs. It took a long time before I could admit to the other truths of the situation, which included sadness, loneliness, and yearning for support.

For many of us, admitting to our real dependency is a deeply difficult thing to do, largely because in the process it's inevitable we'll meet the pain that we incurred as dependent children. Despite this, we know deep down that allowing ourselves to be dependent on inanimate objects or activities, whatever they seem to give us in the moment, is no real substitute. As John Donne famously wrote, "No man is an island / Entire of itself…" Therefore the aim, if there is one, is not to become totally independent of everything, including the objects of our addiction. Rather, we learn what it is okay for us to be dependent on and to begin to experience healthy dependency, which includes learning how to trust ourselves and others, listening to the wisdom of our bodies, and opening to the possibilities of true mutual support, love, and interdependence.

By looking in detail for what it is that compels us to use a substance or undertake an activity we're addicted to, we inevitably find ourselves face to face with our true longings. A compulsion to eat chocolate may overlay a need for love or acceptance. A desire for alcohol may be revealed as a desire for approval. All of these are basic human needs, rather than the shameful or unappealing traits we often imagine them to be. What we discover as we keep on inquiring is how okay it is to be healthily dependent on each other. It's okay for us to depend on each other for love, warmth, friendship and security, simply because we're human. We may also discover something beyond all of that: the profound knowing that we can depend on life itself.

On the Miracle of Mind

I mind. I don't mind. Mindful. Mindless. Minding the
shop. Childminding. Mind how you go. Don't mind if I do.
A piece of my mind.

In spiritual circles, the mind is often blamed for our suffering. If only
we could get rid of our ego, we opine, all would be well. If we only
thought positively, or we didn't think at all, or if we just didn't think
stressful thoughts, our lives would be immeasurably improved. The
idea of being thought-free is held as an ideal state. It's an easy notion
to buy into, partly because it's very simplistic—we've identified the
culprit and we know what we're aiming for. Yet what is it that is
buying into this idea other than the mind itself? It identifies itself as
a problem and then sets about trying to find ways to solve itself.

Assuming the mind's existence as a discrete entity, let's take
stock of what it actually does. It has an immensely complicated job
description: administrator, organizer, educator, student, archivist,
retriever of information, creator, direction finder, dreamer, coach,
technician, engineer, philosopher, interpreter of both internal and
external information, linguist, mathematician, communicator,
defender, imaginer, connector, fantasist, and scientist. Every second
of every day it attempts to make sense and meaning out of our experience. More than anything else, the mind *minds*. It does its level
best to look after us and those things and people we care about in
all the ways it knows how.

Given the immense scope of its tasks, it's hardly surprising that
sometimes the mind goes wrong, that it misinterprets or discon-
nects or otherwise malfunctions. At any given moment, the mind

reaches its conclusions based on the information and interpretations available to it at that time. When we come to its deeper reaches in which our perceptions of ourselves, others, and the world were first formed, we find that the data on which it based those conclusions is from childhood. To use a technical analogy, it's like trying to run a modern computer on Windows 1.0. It's simply not going to work, as the basic operating system isn't able to see beyond itself.

Yet the mind can, and sometimes does, open to the notion of examining itself and its very existence. This openness, readiness, or willingness is crucial. Once it is willing, the mind finds ways to explore, to open itself up. Anyone who has explored a spiritual path for long enough to complain about the mind's shortcomings had a mind willing to explore such a path in the first place.

Inquiry gives us a way to test all the mind's hypotheses through a beautiful blend of science and artistry. By using the body's response as our guide, we look at every element—the thoughts, images, sensations, and emotions—to see if that particular hypothesis is correct or not. The hypothesis could be anything from "I'm not good enough and no one will ever love me," to "I'm the best," to "There's something threatening out there I have to protect myself against," to "I have to drink eight coffees a day." Whatever the hypothesis or belief is, inquiry allows us to examine the original data on which our minds came to those conclusions and see if they're still valid.

The key is using the body to question the mind. When we trust our body's responses, we often come to a much deeper knowing or understanding. We come to *know*, deeply in our being, that we're not who or what we thought we were. This level of knowing has little to do with the mind and yet the mind is radically transformed by it. A natural upgrading of the system takes place and the mind is freed from the task of having to operate on and defend wildly out of date or erroneous data. Once freed, it has the energy to do whatever it naturally does best. We become more creative, more authentically ourselves.

As I said, all it takes is a willingness to look. The inquiry process allows our overtaxed, overstressed minds to take their rightful place as willing servant and co-creator, rather than overbearing, and ultimately reluctant, master. The mind and all its minding can then happen in just the way it does, without judgment or shame, and without one aspect of the mind mindlessly attacking another. In my experience, the mind's openness to question itself and its most dearly held beliefs are among its most precious gifts. For that, and for all its other miracles, I am truly grateful.

On the End of Hope as We Know It

One cold, March day, I watched as hope crumbled. I sat on my sofa, music playing, and hope died. I cried, I wrote, I was amazed at how much had been veiled by hope. I'd wanted to believe in something, anything, so badly. Hope had given me something to hold onto, a place to stand. Doing the Living Inquiries and being willing to look at all my beliefs, all those places I stood, had left me with precisely nowhere to stand, and thus hope fell.

Hope gets good press. Hope makes it onto the front of greetings cards, into songs, even into presidential campaigns. It speaks of brighter, bolder futures. Hope's narratives are compelling. I used to live on hope, like many of us do. I hoped so hard. I hoped that it wasn't really like this. I hoped it would get better. I hoped I would get better.

Yet, the day that hope died, I felt immense relief. The giving up of hope also meant the end of illusion. Hope meant forever leaving here and journeying beyond now. Hope, innocent, sweet hope, had blinded me many times. And clinging to hope was so exhausting. I saw how hope was a subtle controlling force in its desire for life to go a certain way. I saw that hope holds out the illusion of escape because it holds out for something different, rather than being with this.

The sweetest of surrenders came once hope was no more. A merciful giving up to this, here, now. I saw that there was nothing to be rejected, excluded, or avoided. A resounding *yes* came from the depths of my being. There was exquisite beauty and profound gratitude because the end of hope didn't mean hopelessness, as I'd always feared, but something so much vaster and all-encompassing that was way beyond both hope and hopelessness.

We experience these sublime moments, these precious insights, and life continues. I haven't stopped hoping. It's a natural human response, particularly to the pain and suffering of ourselves and others. If you're ill, I hope you feel better soon. If it's your birthday, I hope you have a happy one. I'm sure there are times and places in which hope is life-sustaining.

A few days ago, I found myself experiencing the hope that comes when we want something to go our way for more self-centered reasons. I wanted a response from a close friend whom I feared I may have upset. When I didn't receive it, I was surprised by the intensity of feeling that came. As I stayed with the feeling, I touched a deep well of despair. *What is the point? How the fuck is life supposed to work?* The despair came, I sobbed, and I saw the last strand of remaining hope—a little bit of hope that has been hanging on since the tragic death of my best friend when we were eighteen years old. The hope that something would work, that someone would come and look after me, that this despair would change, that I'd be able to avoid it somehow. As I finally felt the despair, relief came again. The relief that comes with such raw honesty. The relief of not having to lie any more. Clarity came with the end of hope, as I was able to see what was actually here.

Here's the thing: we've been led to believe that we *should* hope. As if it's always a virtue. As if it makes us better people. In reality, it can be just another way to not face what's here, to avoid despair or grief or whatever lies beneath. Questioning the value of hope can feel transgressive. As I said, it's not that hope is wrong. Not at all, in the right circumstance. But what is our hoping really doing? Is hope obscuring our view? Are we hoping that our loved one will change in the face of glaring evidence to the contrary? Are we clinging onto hope so that we don't have to face the reality of our situation? Is hope actually preventing us from taking the action we need to take?

We may even feel that the act of hoping itself will make things happen, that somehow if we didn't hope, nothing would improve and nothing would change. As if good things only come to those who hope. The idea of not having hope may seem frightening if we believe that hope itself—which is made up of words, images of what we'd like to happen in the future, and bodily sensations—is determining the course of our lives in some way and that without it we'd stay stuck. What we discover when we look more deeply is that being with what's actually here catalyzes transformation in a much more profound way than hoping our way out of our situation.

As Dante wrote in *The Divine Comedy*, "Abandon all hope, you who enter here." Inquiring dismantles all our sacred cows. With hope as we have known it abandoned, we find ourselves not in Dante's entrance to hell, but right here in the present moment, just as it is. Here, it's possible we may discover more than we ever dared hope for, in the midst of what we've been hoping to avoid.

On Looking Beneath Behavior

We've all done it. We behave in a way that feels painful, or is destructive, or think we shouldn't, and we resolve to behave differently in the future. We believe that the way to change behavior A is to take up behavior B. What we discover is that, however fervently we wish to change our behavior, it's not that easy. We can't just drop behavior A just because we've decided to for whatever reason.

Whatever behavior A is—smoking, drinking alcohol, getting angry, eating too much, not eating enough, spending too much, criticizing others, and whatever behavior B is—usually the opposite of behavior A, we're convinced that our repeated failure to move from one to the other is evidence of weakness, dysfunction, or incapacity. As Einstein famously said, "Insanity is doing the same thing over and over again and expecting a different result." "This time," we tell ourselves, "it will be different." Occasionally, it is. Most often, it isn't and we find ourselves back on the same old treadmill yet again.

Convinced that the only way to change our behavior is to behave differently, we miss the fact that how we behave is not really the issue. This is not to suggest in any way that our behavior doesn't have consequences. Of course it does, both for ourselves and for others. But the real issue is what drives our behavior. What comes prior to the cigarette, or the evening spent sitting on the sofa stuffing our faces with food and television?

Before I met Scott Kiloby, I had developed some basic understanding that looking more deeply at our unresolved issues is the key to changing our behavior. Some old patterns had shifted, and I no longer smoked or criticized myself quite so harshly. However, I'd never learned how to look so deeply and specifically as we do in the

Living Inquiries. And it turned out that the devil really is in the details.

I'll give a personal example. In my late teens and early twenties, I developed moderate bulimia. I say "moderate" because although I didn't induce vomiting or take laxatives, I did alternately binge and starve. I was, however, obsessed with food intake and body image. Staggering as it seems now in the internet age, I had no idea that what I was experiencing had a name. It wasn't until I was twenty-two and through the worst of it that I read about bulimia in *Cosmopolitan* magazine. It was a revelation to discover that other women and men had this, too. I'd never discussed it with another soul and it was some time before I did so.

While the outward behaviors of bingeing and starving fell away after a few years, the inner patterns remained. For a long time, I believed that my only recourse was to be resolute, to use my will-power to control and manage the inner urges. On one level, I was successful. I never did go back to the worst excesses of the binge-and-starve cycle. But as anyone who has controlled an addiction or compulsion through sheer effort and force of will knows, it takes a huge effort to do so. Because the basic pattern, the obsession itself, remains more or less intact.

My attention returns to looking at my food and body image issues every once in a while. Now in my mid-fifties and with a changing body, it has been challenging to find myself putting on a few extra pounds. My first response was to, you've guessed it, change my behavior. I thought it all through: I'd eat less, exercise more, and set targets for myself.

We can get so wrapped up in all that activity that we lose sight of the fact that we'll simply be doing more of the same and expect-ing a different outcome—yet more insanity. I resolved to stop eating sugar for a while and did so. I spent a few weeks feeling the glow of the righteous abstainer, until I stepped on the scale and discovered that I'd actually put on more weight. Shocked, I dropped the idea of *doing* anything else and started to really look deeply.

That same day, I began to feel the sensations and feelings that had arisen when I'd seen the number on the scale. Staying with them for a while, a memory emerged from my first year in senior school. I was in the staff section of the school cafeteria, having volunteered to clear up after the teachers had finished their lunch. One of the perks of volunteering was eating their leftovers. As I looked at the memory, emotion welled and I went with it. Then words came, "I'm still that girl." More emotion followed and the looking continued.

We often find that a relatively small number of images, words, and feelings hold a whole pattern of behavior in place. In my case, looking at the memory of the school cafeteria gave me access to long-suppressed feelings from that time in my life. It became clear just how the cycle had begun in the first place. I spent time with that twelve-year-old girl, utterly bewildered by events happening around her over which she had no control.

Since then, I've kept inquiring into these and related issues by myself and with facilitators. As I've looked, my behavior has changed naturally and without effort. I still haven't eaten any sweet food, yet I do not have any sense of denying myself anything. I've bought new clothes for the first time in a long while, clothes that I feel good about myself in and that reflect who I am now. And I've marveled at how, when we stop, rest, and inquire, change happens. We simply find ourselves behaving differently. Transformation occurs not because we make it so, but because we're willing to look and feel.

On the Violence of the Deficiency Story

Inquiring into our deficiency stories isn't about navel-gazing, solipsism, or feeling better about ourselves. It has a real-world effect in our lives and on the people around us.

The belief that we're deficient does violence to both ourselves and others. Whether that violence manifests through self-shaming or self-harming, addictions, belittling others, using knives or guns, it arises from the stories we have about ourselves and the world around us. Behind each and every act of violence, from the subtle to the outright horrific, lies an unexamined story of deficiency. "I'm powerless" or "I'm threatened" or "I'm a victim" or "I'm superior or inferior." Whatever the exact flavor of the story that's running, it can only end badly, sometimes over and over again as we repeat the same patterns.

When our deficiency stories run unchecked or unnoticed, they color our every interaction and every relationship. In fact, the deeper the story runs, the further its tentacles spread. The more separate and lacking the self feels, the more it projects itself into everything, and the more violent its actions become.

We see the endpoint of this in states of mental illness, including the paranoid schizophrenic who sees innocent passersby as agents of the state, or the psychopath who is incapable of perceiving that others have a different set of opinions and emotions. I once knew a young woman who had been horrifically abused in childhood and she not only dangerously and repeatedly self-harmed, but also believed that she was responsible for both world wars.

The more painful the deficiency, the more skewed our boundaries become. While most of us don't fall into the extremes, we all experience the world through our own deficiency lenses. It's natural that our deficiency stories arise as they do in response to the circumstances of our early lives. We don't have any control over their formation (so we don't need to feel deficient about having deficiency stories). The stories, painful in themselves, are paradoxically a way to attempt to avoid feeling our deepest pain or keeping it safely encapsulated. In fact, the more painful the identity, the more self there seems to be and the denser and stickier the knot of thoughts and bodily feelings that seems to make up the self becomes. It's as if the size of the self is in direct proportion to the pain contained therein.

This mechanism of being a self with a story isn't particularly efficient at keeping the pain at bay and we find ourselves regularly triggered and acting out, harming ourselves or others in the process. Sometimes the damage is minimal, consisting of some yelling perhaps or a bout of overeating. At other times, the damage is much more substantial—we're all aware of the many shades of violence that we humans collectively inflict on ourselves and the world around us.

So what happens when we inquire? We get gut-level honest about what is actually happening. We stay with our immediate experience and begin to notice what's here—the various thoughts (words and mental images) and feelings (emotions, sensations, and other bodily energies) that make up the particular deficiency story that we're investigating.

We move from blaming others ("outward pointing," as Scott calls it) to seeing that our perception is colored by the belief that we're unlovable, or unwanted, or worthless. This is not to say that we deny the pain that others have caused us or that we blame ourselves in any way. Far from it. We meet the pain that's bound up in the deficiency and, in doing so, the story begins to lose its sway. The more we connect with and integrate the pain, the less the deficiency story is required. As we continue to look, we no longer identify as flawed, damaged, or unsafe. Even more to the point, we're freed of the burden of behaving as if we're flawed, damaged, unsafe, or according to our particular brand of deficiency.

The changes that seeing through our deficiency stories brings about cannot be understated. Those acts of violence, large and small, to others and to ourselves, begin to wane. The endless self-criticism or self-shaming begins to quiet. The need for our loved ones or anyone else to be different in some way lessens. When we no longer have a deficiency story to prove or deny, we can simply be ourselves, however we are in each moment. Without a deficiency story, the projections cease. The world, in all its manifestations, is free to be itself and freed of the burden of meaning something to or about us.

Afterword

The Living Inquiries leave us with nowhere to land. When we're willing to look at every aspect of our experience, particularly at what seems to keep us separate, we find that we can no longer hold fast to anything.

At times, this can feel deeply uncomfortable. Ultimately, it is very freeing. Despite the fears that inevitably arise—we'll cease to exist, or that we won't be able to function if we're no longer the person that we've believed ourselves to be—we discover, time and time again, that life doesn't require us to conform to our beliefs. In fact, life invites us to look beyond our beliefs in every moment.

The invitation to look can come in a variety of ways. Some of us reach a point at which our lives simply don't work anymore and the self that we've taken ourselves to be starts to fall apart, writhing in dysfunction. Others may have fleetingly glimpsed oneness, how life is beyond the conceptual veil, and want to return there. Sometimes it's simply that we've had enough of suffering and have tried all the alternatives to no avail. Only when every other option has been exhausted do we give up the hope of finding better in the future and begin to look more closely at exactly what is here and now.

As you've read, inquiring in this way is totally open-ended. It does not require us to start from a particular standpoint, as we begin with whatever is showing up in the moment. It also doesn't prescribe where we're supposed to end up. There is no teaching or pointing involved, nothing to understand intellectually, nowhere to get to, no specific result to achieve. Every session is different. There may well be revelations, insights, or realizations along the way, along with releases of emotion and disentangling of beliefs, but the process is allowed to take whatever course it takes, wherever it goes.

The key lies in our willingness to look at everything. The teachings of non-duality used to appeal to me because I liked the idea of getting rid of this troublesome, painful self. Rather than transcending the painful and troublesome self, inquiring takes us right into it. Contrary to our usual expectation, it is right in the midst of what we've taken to be pain and suffering that freedom is discovered. Inquiring takes us so far beyond the conceptual that ideas about self, no self, or anything else, become totally moot.

What does *freedom* really mean? As we inquire, we become freer of the habitual, conditioned responses and beliefs that have previously shaped our lives. We find that we can move beyond our compulsions and addictions because we're no longer trying to manage or dull our pain. We're less limited by anxiety, fear, and the effects of trauma because we no longer perceive ourselves to be in danger or under threat. We're free of the need to defend or protect our view or image of ourselves, because we no longer have one.

When we're willing to look, we let go of the idea of how life should be and begin to experience it as it is. Life's paradoxes become a source of amazement and wonder; the less we find, the fuller life gets. The less solid and real we believe ourselves to be, the more truly ourselves we become. We discover how utterly and innocently mistaken we've been about so many things; we're not what we've believed ourselves to be and neither is anything else.

The Inquiries are also deeply humbling. We face all those parts of ourselves that we've tried to hide or compensate for. We encounter shame, anger, grief, humiliation, fear, sadness, and all the other feelings that we've tried not to feel. As we do so, we begin to at last appreciate our naked, human vulnerability. We come to embrace our collective humanity in a profound way; love and compassion arise naturally in the course of inquiring, rendering us open to all that is here.

This is not about having a one-time, moment-of-grace awakening. Those happen, of course. But for many of us, precious and transformative as those moments are, they're really only the beginning. They come and they go, just as any other experience does.

What really counts is our ability and willingness to be fully awake and alive to each moment, whatever it contains. The Living Inquiries develop our capacity to do exactly that, so we're able to be with whatever is here, from the sublime to the excruciatingly painful.

As Scott Kiloby emphasizes, it's in everyday life that the rubber meets the road. If we find ourselves in conflict with others, a deficiency story is running. If we're in the grip of addiction or compulsion, there is some identification with a self happening. If we're anxious or fearful, there is an assumption—however subtle—of a threatened subject within and an external threatening object. If we're willing to look at all of it, what was previously unconscious can be brought into the light of awareness. Rather than resting on the laurels of a past awakening, we're fully present to whatever is here right now.

Our capacity to deepen into life is infinite, just like life itself. We can inquire no matter how life is manifesting, whatever challenges or joys we face. Living the Inquiries takes us deep into the heart of being and allows all that has been unconscious and unlived to bloom and thrive. When we're able to drop our demands for life to be as we want it to be and are able to be with it as it is, our suffering ceases. It's finally okay to be exactly as we are.

Acknowledgments

My heartfelt love and thanks go to Scott Kiloby and Julianne Eanniello. I'm also deeply grateful to everyone in the Living Inquiries community—senior facilitators (both past and present), certified facilitators, and trainees—for all the looking and deepening that we're doing together. Every day, I'm in awe of the courage and willingness of my clients to look so deeply. My thanks to you all—without you, this book would not have been written. Finally, huge gratitude and love to Joah, who makes me laugh so much and so often.

Resources

Fiona Robertson's Websites

Living Inquiries: http://www.beyondourbeliefs.org

Poetry: http://www.whilstwalkingjack.blogspot.com

Twitter: https://www.twitter.com/@fionauk2

Facebook: https://www.facebook.com/fiona.robertson.961

Websites for More Information

The Living Inquiries: http://www.livinginquiries.com, https://www
.facebook.com/groups/livinginquirires.scottkiloby/

Natural Rest for Addiction: http://www.naturalrestforaddiction
.com, https://www.facebook.com/groups/naturalrestforaddiction/

Scott Kiloby: http://www.kiloby.com

The Kiloby Center for Recovery: http://www.kilobycenter.com

The creators of the Living Inquiries include Scott Kiloby, Fiona
Robertson, Colette Kelso, Julianne Eanniello, and the senior
facilitators.

Fiona Robertson is a senior facilitator and trainer of Scott Kiloby's Living Inquiries. She works with clients and trainees from around the world using this gentle, radical, and transformative method. She cocreated the Anxiety Inquiry, and is editor of two books by Scott Kiloby. Robertson lives in Nottingham, UK, and occasionally writes poetry.

Foreword writer **Scott Kiloby** is a noted author, teacher, and international speaker on the subject of non-dual wisdom as it applies to addiction, depression, anxiety, and trauma. He is founder of a worldwide community of Living Inquiries facilitators who work with people in over twelve different countries. He is also cofounder of the Kiloby Center for Recovery in Rancho Mirage, CA, the first addiction, anxiety, and depression treatment center to focus primarily on mindfulness.

MORE BOOKS from NON-DUALITY PRESS

BE WHO YOU ARE
Jean Klein

ISBN: 978-0955176258 | US $15.95

WHO AM I?
THE SACRED QUEST
Jean Klein
Compiled and edited by Emma Edwards

ISBN: 978-0955176265 | US $17.95

FIRING GOD

Cheryl Abram

ISBN: 978-1-908664488 | US $14.95

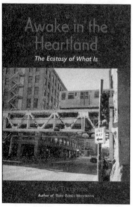

Awake in the Heartland
The Ecstasy of What Is

JOAN TOLLIFSON
Author of BARE-BONES MEDITATION

ISBN: 978-0955176241 | US $19.95

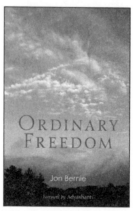

ORDINARY FREEDOM

Jon Bernie

Foreword by Adyashanti

ISBN: 978-0956309198 | US $14.95

THE *Light* that I am
NOTES FROM THE GROUND OF BEING

J.C. Amberchele

ISBN: 978-0955829093 | US $14.95

NON-DUALITY PRESS
An Imprint of New Harbinger Publications
www.newharbinger.com